Steve —

It is great to work

Enjoy this book; It is my favorite

golf book! Enjoy the game of golf!.

Bless You! T.Z.

8-24-12

"For those who have learned that golf is more than just a game, The Mulligan will be welcome reading that will provide helpful insights not just for their golf game, but for their lives as well."

—Ben Crenshaw, two-time Masters Champion and
2002 inductee to the World Golf Hall of Fame

"Wally Armstrong and Ken Blanchard not only understand golf but life and the value of relationships. They have put together a story that should warm your heart, help your golf game, and just may touch your life."

—Jack Nicklaus, golf legend and 1974 inductee
to the World Golf Hall of Fame

"I really enjoyed reading The Mulligan and I know my dad, Harvey, would have loved this simple little book because there are so many things in it that embody the wisdom, grace, and the importance of friendships my dad always treasured."

—Tinsley Penick, PGA golf professional

"A compelling story about the importance of a mulligan. It may only happen on the first tee in golf, but in the game of life it is there for the asking, provided you are prepared to ask and know the One who has the answer."

—C. William Pollard, Chairman of The ServiceMaster
Company and author of The Soul of the Firm

"If you want to improve your golf game and your life, reading The Mulligan is a must. It's a spiritual journey down the fairway."

—John C. Maxwell, author, speaker, and founder
of INJOY Stewardship and EQUIP

"Every now and then we need a wake-up call to remind us of the things in life that really matter. Thankfully, Wally Armstrong and Ken Blanchard in their book, The Mulligan, reassure us that second chances to correct our wrongs are just one swing away!"

—Paul J. Meyer, New York Times best-selling author and f
ounder of Success Motivation International, Inc.

"In The Mulligan, Wally Armstrong and Ken Blanchard strike a common chord among sportsmen and those seeking a better understanding of the broader arena that is life itself. The lessons of second chances, forgiveness, and love are eternal as espoused by the great 'Old Pro' himself: Jesus Christ."

—Pete McDaniel, best-selling author
and senior writer for Golf Digest

"As we walk the fairways of life, this great game teaches us early on that if we continue in our dedication to perfection, good things may happen. The same holds true in our own lives; dedication, hard work, and trial and error will be rewarded. The Mulligan sets the stage for that perfect score. Great job, Wally and Ken!"

—Jerry Rich, owner of Richard Harvest Farms,
site of the 2009 Solheim Cup

"If golf is a metaphor for life, then a mulligan is a perfect metaphor for God's love. Ken Blanchard's new book is a terrific reminder that whenever we ask, God gives us second chances throughout our lives and straight into eternity."

—Bill Jones III, chairman and CEO of Sea Island Company{

"Everyone needs the ultimate mulligan. This book will tell you how to get it. Your life will never be the same. Thanks, Ken and Wally."

—Larry Moody, President of Search Ministries
and pastor to PGA tour players

THE
MULLIGAN

A Parable of Second Chances

THE
MULLIGAN

KEN BLANCHARD

—— AND ——

WALLY ARMSTRONG

ZONDERVAN.com/
AUTHORTRACKER
follow your favorite authors

ZONDERVAN

The Mulligan
Copyright © 2010 by Wally Armstrong and Polvera Publishing

This title is also available as a Zondervan ebook. Visit www.zondervan.com/ebooks.

This title is also available in a Zondervan audio edition. Visit www.zondervan.fm.

Requests for information should be addressed to:

Zondervan, *Grand Rapids, Michigan 49530*

Library of Congress Cataloging-in-Publication Data

Blanchard, Ken, 1939-
      The mulligan : a parable of second chances / Ken Blanchard, Wally
    Armstrong, Kevin G. Harney.
         p. cm.
      ISBN 978-0-310-32814-8 (hardcover, jacketed) 1. Golf — Psychological
    aspects. 2. Golfers — Conduct of life. 3. Golfers — Religious life. I. Armstrong,
    Wally. II. Harney, Kevin G., 1962- III. Title.
    GV979.P75B53 2010
    796.352 — dc22   2010005800

Cover design: Rob Monacelli
Cover Photography: Terzes Photography
Interior design: Matthew Van Zomeren

Printed in the United States of America

10 11 12 13 14 15 /DCI/ 20 19 18 17 16 15 14 13 12 11 10 9 8 7 6 5 4 3 2 1

This book is dedicated to Harvey Penick, Davis Love Jr., and all the Old Pros who teach us about golf and life.

Contents

mulligan (*n*) — In friendly play, permission granted a golfer by the other players to retake a flubbed shot, especially the first shot of the game. Golf's generous forgiveness, The Mulligan originated in the United States at the Winged Foot Golf Club and was created by David B. Mulligan. This second-chance shot is not allowed by the official rules of golf.

CHAPTER I

THE EXECUTIVE

"LATE AS USUAL," Paul McAllister grumbled to himself as he sped toward the Biltmore Forest Country Club in Asheville, North Carolina. He'd flown in yesterday from Atlanta, and being late for his tee-off time for the Pro-Am was the last thing he wanted to be. Playing in this tournament was something he had wanted to do for a long time. He was especially excited about it after last night's Pro-Am Pairing Party, when his foursome had drawn Davis Love III. Year after year, Love was one of the greatest players on the PGA golf tour. His late father, Davis Love Jr., had been revered as one of the best teachers of the game anywhere.

What an opportunity, thought McAllister. *Maybe Love can help me with my golf game.*

Paul's attitude toward golf was the same attitude he had toward everything: he wanted to be the best. At forty-five, Paul saw life as one achievement game after another.

He had gone to an Ivy League school, working hard to make sure he ranked near the top of his class. He became president or captain of everything he joined. Everything for him was about getting ahead. Get into a good graduate school. Land a job with the best possible company. Stay one step in front of the next guy. Paul McAllister was driven — and he was very successful.

The only failure Paul ever had was his marriage. Right after he earned his MBA he married Rebecca, his college sweetheart. She was one of the most popular girls on campus.

Everybody wanted her, but he beat out the competition. He secretly enjoyed the fact that if he had fumbled his lines at the wedding ceremony, at least three of the guys in his wedding party would have stepped forward to take his place. Once the ceremony was over, Paul figured the marriage job was done. Now he could get back to work.

After five years of trying to find some way of being part of Paul's life, including having a son, Rebecca filed for divorce. She tried everything — even suggesting marriage counseling — but Paul never had time. It wasn't important to him. He was too busy being an entrepreneur and building his business. After working for a great company for two years he had decided to go out on his own. He worked harder than ever. But there were consequences. Just as Paul had predicted, the marriage job was done. His wife and child were out of his life. And though there was some initial pain and regret, Paul took it as a career-enhancing opportunity.

Free to focus on the business he started three years before, Paul grew it into a multimillion dollar operation. When Paul looked at his life, he thought real success had to do with the amount of wealth he accumulated, the amount of recognition he got for his efforts, and the power and status he achieved. But after fifteen years of experiencing the momentary highs from making one hot deal after another, Paul felt something was missing. It was not enough.

Even though people who grew up with Paul — like the classmates he saw at his twenty-fifth year high school reunion — viewed him as being very successful, that did not comfort him. No matter what he achieved, it never was enough. The job was never done. Instead of slowing down to find out why, Paul was always looking for the next mountain to climb. And for Paul, that next mountain was golf.

Golf became the second singular passion in Paul's life. Golf was the one connection he had shared with his functioning alcoholic father. Paul's happiest memories were of walking the public course near their home on late summer afternoons with his dad, who took off work early to teach him the game. When Paul was twelve, his dad was killed in a car accident — ending that shining period. From that day forward Paul felt abandoned and alone. His life was an unending mission to fill the void.

CHAPTER 2

A TRAUMA

PAUL CAME RACING into the clubhouse parking lot and frowned as he stopped the car—no one was waiting to take his bag. When a youngster finally showed up, Paul was short with him. Giving the kid his bag, Paul hurried off to the registration desk without giving him a tip. After registering, he realized that he had only thirty minutes until his tee-off time. *Not much time to warm up*, Paul thought. He headed quickly to the driving range to beat as many balls as possible before he had to go to the first tee.

Waiting for him at the tee were three other amateurs, whom Paul had met at the Pairing Party the night before. But after finding out what they did for a living and whom they didn't know, he wrote them off as not being important enough to get to know. As a result, he shook their hands in a cursory way. His main concern was the whereabouts of their pro member, Davis Love III.

Just as the starter asked if the 11:30 group was ready to go, Love walked through the crowd and onto the tee. He had a warm smile on his face as he introduced himself to each of his amateur playing partners.

As Paul shook Davis's hand he was wondering how he could make Love realize that *he* was the most important member of the group. Paul had taken a number of lessons during the last three weeks in preparation for this tournament. Maybe his golf game would pave the way to a relationship with Love.

Attempting to be gracious, Paul encouraged his three playing partners to hit first after Love sent a towering drive from the back tee down the middle of the fairway well over three hundred yards away. As Paul watched his playing partners hit their drives, a small grin appeared on his face. He realized these guys were real hackers — twenty handicappers at best. And here he was, a twelve handicapper who would soon be a single-digit player.

When it came Paul's turn to hit, he walked confidently to the tee box, teed up his ball, and stepped back to look up the fairway toward the hole. His caddy broke in, "The best spot to hit your drive on this hole is the right center of the fairway. It opens up the hole from there, especially given where they've set the pin today." The caddy's advice broke Paul's concentration. *I hope he is not going to talk in my ear all day*, thought Paul. *I know how to play this game.*

With that he stepped up to the ball, swung too hard, and hit a wild hook. Not only did it not end up on the right side of the fairway, but it landed in heavy rough on the left. He glanced quickly around the gallery to see if there was anybody taking any pictures that he could blame. He'd seen top pros do this many times on TV. But when he looked in Davis's direction, the pro wasn't paying attention. He didn't seem to care where Paul's shot had gone.

Paul's hook off the first tee was a sign of things to come. He went from bad to worse. While his higher-handicap playing partners were short off the tee, they were straight and kept on bogeying holes. Paul, on the other hand, hit his tee shots long but they were wild. He ended up contributing double bogeys. He picked up on more holes than he finished. Paul did everything he could to fix his swing, but nothing seemed to work. As they reached the ninth hole, Paul really was losing it: he wasn't developing a relationship with Love and he wasn't having fun.

Paul's negative self-talk began to take over, as usual.

You idiot, he thought. *This is embarrassing! How can you play like this? Those lessons certainly didn't help.*

When it came his turn to tee off, Paul quieted his mind for the first time during the round and lo and behold, he hit a perfect drive that brought a smile to his face. *Now I am going to get it together*, he thought. He followed his drive with a beautiful four iron that bounced on the center of the green and stopped four feet from the cup. Even the crowd gathered around the green waiting to see Davis Love applauded Paul as he approached.

After Davis and his playing partners had putted out, it was Paul's turn. Paul's heart was racing. Since this was the number-two-handicap hole on the card, he got a stroke. If he could make this birdie putt, it would mean an eagle for his team. Davis Love knew that and helped Paul read the putt. But when he stroked the ball it came up three inches short of the cup—the dreaded "never up, never in."

Paul clenched his teeth and felt his face grow hot with anger. Tapping the ball into the cup for par, he completely lost it. He took his putter and without even thinking, snapped it over his knee. Everybody around him—including the caddies—slowly walked away in silence, leaving him alone on the green.

Paul didn't know whether to cry or yell. It suddenly struck him that now he would have to putt the rest of the round with a two iron or a wood. What he had hoped would be a wonderful day had turned into a nightmare.

When Paul finally headed for the tenth tee, Davis Love was waiting for him.

"Paul," he said in a caring voice, "we haven't talked much during the first nine holes, but I've been watching you. And to be honest, you aren't good enough to get that mad. What you just did on the ninth green may have as much to say about where you are with your life as your game. Think about it." With that, Love headed to the tee to hit his shot.

Love's comments froze Paul in his tracks. He was deeply embarrassed — probably for the first time in his life (at least that he would admit). He wondered if he should just quit and walk to his car. But Love's remarks had hooked him. They made him want to stay.

Walking down from the tenth tee, Paul waited for Love to catch up. Love hit his drive from the back tee, almost seventy-five yards farther than where the amateurs hit. As Love walked up, Paul was almost too choked up to speak.

"What you said to me," Paul finally managed, "hit me like a ton of bricks. I apologize. I've been a real jerk."

CHAPTER 3

THE MENTOR

As Paul followed him down the fairway, Love said, "That's okay, Paul. I've played in a lot of Pro-Ams. It's hard watching what people do to themselves on the golf course. I make a living playing golf and you make a living doing something else, but what we do on the golf course often reflects how we live our lives. My father always taught me that life and golf have a lot in common. In fact, Dad used to say that golf spells **G**ame **O**f **L**ife **F**irst."

Paul laughed for the first time during the round. "I always heard this game was called golf because all the other four-letter words were taken. But now that I think about it, I like your acronym better than my joke."

"So do I," said Davis with a smile. "If he were still alive, I would suggest you go see my father. Not only was he a great teacher of the game of golf, he was a great teacher of the game of life. But there is an old friend of his who

I think could really help you. Everyone who knows him calls him the Old Pro. His name is Willie Dunn.

"The Old Pro," Love continued, "was named after his grandfather, Old Willie Dunn. He was a famous Scottish golf course designer and teacher in the mid-1800s. His father, John Duncan Dunn, was a golf professional and came over to the United States in 1898 to teach and design golf courses in Florida and California. So with a family background like that, Willie won his share of trophies until his competitive playing career ended tragically from a shoulder wound during World War II. After the war, he settled in Asheville, North Carolina, and he's been teaching golf here for over sixty years.

"I think you'll find him on the porch by the clubhouse at the end of the round," Davis continued. "He loves to sit there and watch golfers come and go — watch life go by. Willie is almost ninety now, but he's as sharp as a tack and one of the wisest men I know. I recommend you spend some time with him. Tell him I sent you."

After talking to Davis, Paul was amazed how relaxed he felt over the back nine. And guess what? He played better from tee to green and hit some incredible shots, as much as it was embarrassing to putt with his three wood for the entire back nine. Even though Davis's words had been hard to hear, Paul realized he was right. Here he was, grinding his teeth over a game he didn't spend that much time perfecting. Yet he expected outstanding performance on every shot! He also thought about the relationship between golf and life and realized he was feeling down about both right now.

Maybe I need a mulligan, Paul thought.

The idea surprised him. Paul had always been a stickler for enforcing rules, so he'd never really liked the common practice of granting players another shot off the first tee, without penalty, if their initial drive was not to their liking. Despite the fact that Paul had been in situations where he could have offered a fellow player a mulligan or could have accepted one for himself, he did neither. His pride would never let him accept charity or give it. Nevertheless, he had really blown the chance of a lifetime today. He would have loved to play the front nine over again without any consequences. It would have been a whole different experience. He smiled as he visualized a mulligan first nine. *That would be the ultimate mulligan*, he thought.

Paul laughed, recalling his first visit to Scotland. It was there he learned that hitting a mulligan requires the goodwill of those with whom you are playing.

The first Scottish course he played was Turnberry, where the British Open had been held several times. When Paul's playing partner hit his initial drive into the rough, he turned to the starter and asked, "Could I have a mulligan?" Without changing his expression the starter said, "If you take a mulligan in Scotland, you are shooting three."

Paul's thoughts returned to the final round of the day's Pro-Am. When it was over, Paul shook hands with his team members and walked quietly over to Davis.

Pointing up at the porch, Davis said, "The Old Pro's there. You can't miss him. He's sitting in the rocker to the far left."

"Thanks for your help and advice," Paul said.

"Good luck. I have a hunch the Old Pro will help you with more than just your golf game."

CHAPTER 4

A NEW LEASE ON LIFE

AFTER HIS CADDY CLEANED HIS CLUBS and sent them to the parking lot to be placed in his car, Paul headed toward the clubhouse. As he approached, he saw the Old Pro sitting in the rocker. He was wearing knickers and argyle socks. The wrinkles on the back of his neck were deep and crisscrossed, like a roadmap that had been folded over and over again. Paul was struck by the warm smile on the man's face. He smiled back and said, "Davis Love said I ought to talk to you."

The Old Pro smiled. "Sit down, son," he said.

Taking a seat, Paul asked, "What should I call you, sir?"

"Just call me Will," said the old man.

"Okay, Will, that sounds good to me," said Paul.

"What did you do out there, son, that Davis sent you my way?"

"Well, sir, I think I was taking the game too seriously, just like I always do. I was trying to impress Love and my teammates with my ability, but hit an ugly shot off the first tee. Then things went from bad to worse. Finally, on the ninth hole, I hit a great drive and a beautiful second shot four feet from the cup. I had an opportunity to get an eagle for my team and I didn't even get the putt to the hole!"

"Remember what Yogi Berra said," said the Old Pro. " 'Ninety percent of the putts that are short don't go in.' Seriously, lots of people leave important putts short. So you didn't make the putt. Is that the whole story?" the Old Pro asked with a knowing look in his eyes.

Paul took a deep breath and continued, "No. What I did next was way out of line. I just lost it and snapped my putter over my knee. On the next hole Davis spoke to me privately about my explosion on the ninth green. He said I wasn't good enough to get that mad and that my behavior might have as much to say about my life as it did about my game."

The Old Pro gave Paul a sympathetic smile.

"What Davis told me cut me to the core. Do you have time to talk?" asked Paul.

The Old Pro said slowly in a caring way, "All the time in the world, son."

"Davis said that you could help straighten out my life as well as my golf game."

"That's a tall order," said the Old Pro. "But golf and life do have a great deal in common. Golf has a way of showing what is going on inside someone. As Davis probably told you, his father and I agreed that to master the game of golf you have to master the **G**ame **O**f **L**ife **F**irst."

"He mentioned that," said Paul. "Could you tell me more?"

"Sure," said the Old Pro with a smile. "In life, as in golf:

- You get good breaks you deserve.
- You get good breaks you don't deserve.
- You get bad breaks you deserve.
- You get bad breaks you don't deserve.
- Sometimes you are performing or playing better than you should and you have to deal with success.
- Sometimes you are performing or playing worse than you should and you have to deal with failure.

"In golf this all takes place in four-and-a-half hours with that little ball staring at you and nobody there to hit it but yourself. In life it occurs every moment of every day."

"That's interesting," said Paul. "I never thought of it that way."

The Old Pro smiled. "My last name is Dunn, so I like to think that maybe at the end of my life I will hear, 'Well done, Will Dunn!'"

Not understanding the gist of the Old Pro's humor, Paul responded, "So can you help teach me the game of life?"

"Son, *life is all about relationships.* We have to get to know each other. That means we need to spend some time together. When are you going to get back this way?"

"As soon as possible," said Paul. "In fact, maybe I could stay over until tomorrow. What's your schedule?" Paul couldn't believe he'd said that. Relationships just weren't his thing. But the embarrassment he felt about breaking his putter in front of Davis Love III had been a significant emotional event — what some people might call "a cosmic goose." Paul thought that maybe getting close to the Old Pro would give him a chance to redeem himself with Love.

The Old Pro said, "At my age, son, I don't like to get up at the crack of dawn anymore. Why don't we meet at the Muni at ten o'clock tomorrow morning."

"What's the Muni?" asked Paul.

"That's the municipal course on the other side of Asheville. It's not as fancy as this place but it works just fine. It's where I learned the game of golf and the game of life."

Shaking the Old Pro's hand, Paul said, "Thanks. See you tomorrow at ten."

CHAPTER 5

REFLECTION

PAUL SPENT A THOUGHTFUL DINNER by himself that night. It had really gotten to him when the Old Pro said, "Life is all about relationships." Deep down inside, something was waking up in Paul that had been buried long ago. But before he could remember what it was, his skeptical side kicked in.

Is this man for real? Can I really trust him? thought Paul. He certainly could never count on his father. He never knew which father he was going to get. Would it be the one he enjoyed playing golf with — or the abusive drunk who was critical of everything he did? Paul was always looking for that little ounce of praise. But it never came. His dad died when Paul needed him most.

Later in his teen years, Paul was drawn to the basketball coach at his school. The coach befriended him and even taught him to play golf again. Paul idolized him, but then he abandoned Paul. The coach left town with a fair-haired teacher he'd been secretly having an affair with. He made no attempt to say good-bye.

After that, Paul decided he couldn't trust anybody but himself. It was best to go it alone in life. His drive to be a superachiever kicked into high gear. He became a "human doing," not a human being, looking to his performance for significance. Relationships were now secondary — even, eventually, his relationship with his son, Jake. Inside Paul was afraid: afraid of getting hurt again by investing too much in his relationships, afraid that if he let his guard down people would see things in him that even he didn't want to admit. That made him vulnerable.

But the Old Pro seemed different somehow. Maybe Paul's life really wasn't working as well as it should, and his golf game could use some help.

Paul stopped into the hotel gift shop after dinner and picked up a journal. *Maybe this will help me keep track of the ideas firing in my mind*, he thought. For years people had told him that journaling was a good process, but he never wanted to do it. If he — a type-A personality — were going to write a journal, he wanted to do it better than anybody else. He knew people who did their journalizing in four colors. Others wrote poetry in their journals. How could he begin to compete with that?

Paul had recently read an article about journaling that suggested a simple, noncompetitive format. The idea was that at the end of the day or early the next morning, you'd write the date at the top of a journal page and start off with a section praising yourself for things you'd done well that day. *I'll call this section "Solid Shots,"* he thought. These were things that made you feel good about yourself because they were consistent with what you had hoped to accomplish or who you wanted to be in the world. Paul wasn't quite sure what to make of the latter. Who he wanted to be in the world was beyond his thinking right now. His only concern was being the best.

The article also suggested that after you praise yourself, you create a section in your journal entitled "Redirection." Underneath would go things from that day you wish you could do over—times when you didn't like the result or the response you got from others. *I think I'll call this section "Mulligans,"* Paul thought. *After all, Davis Love and the Old Pro are telling me that life and golf have a lot in common.*

Later that night as he settled into bed, Paul picked up his journal and wrote the date. Then he began:

•　　•　　•

Il have no idea how this journaling thing works except for the article I read recently. But I'm ready to give it my best shot. Under "Solid Shots" I'll write what I did well that day. Under "Mulligans" I'll try to be honest about where I could make some adjustments and improvements.

Next he wrote:

Solid Shots

I surprised myself being open to Davis's candid comments about the state of my game and my life. I do realize I am not happy about either and I might need some help.

I took the initiative to meet with Willie Dunn and even changed my plans and my flight to stay an extra day in Asheville. I hope it's worth it!

As he considered the "Mulligans" section, Paul laughed. He thought about how he would have loved to replay that whole first nine. *Maybe it's true there are no accidents in life,* he thought. *If I hadn't been such a jerk during the first nine, I wouldn't have the opportunity to spend tomorrow with Will Dunn. Maybe there are reasons for things that are beyond my control.* He smiled as he wrote:

Mulligans

I need another chance at tipping the bag boy and not being rude to him. I also blew it when I ignored my playing partners and my caddy because I was trying to impress Davis Love III.

If that's not bad enough, my golf game stinks. If I could take a big mulligan, why not just take one for the whole front nine today? Now that would be the Ultimate Mulligan. What could be greater than that?

That's it for today. I should probably keep this journal somewhere safe. I don't want someone reading it.

This was new thinking for Paul. It felt foreign. Still, he looked forward to developing a relationship with the Old Pro.

As he drifted off to sleep, Paul reflected that the day had not gone as he had expected, but he sensed it was the beginning of something important.

CHAPTER 6

SOURCE OF
SELF-WORTH

THE NEXT MORNING the receptionist at the hotel gave Paul directions to the Muni course. He headed out about 8:30; he wanted to hit some balls so he would be ready to go when he met the Old Pro at ten. He had never heard of a municipal course called Muni, but this added to the mystique of the Old Pro.

Paul slowed as he approached the course. On the driving range he noticed players in a wide variety of outfits, including jeans and shorts that would not have passed the length test at his private club in Atlanta. Though it did have a public course feeling, the Muni was different from most municipal courses. It appeared to be a well-kept, well-run operation.

The clubhouse was an old stone building, nothing fancy. But as he drove into the parking lot, what really got his attention was the sign that said the course had been designed by Donald Ross. Paul knew enough about the history of golf to know that Ross was one of the greatest golf architects of all time. He had designed hundreds of golf courses, including the famous Pinehurst No. 2, Oakland Hills, and Oak Hill. Courses with his signature on them had hosted many national championships through the years. In fact, the famous Biltmore Forest Golf Club where the Pro-Am was played the day before was one of Ross's masterpieces. But a municipal course in Asheville, North Carolina? That seemed a little strange to Paul.

After he parked his car and got out his golf clubs, Paul bought two large buckets of balls and headed to the range. He had an hour before he was supposed to meet the Old Pro, so he figured he had plenty of time to use up both buckets. He was known to beat balls in rapid-fire succession until his hands hurt. This morning would have been no exception if he hadn't seen the Old Pro sitting in a rocker on the front porch just as he was about to buy more balls to hit.

I wonder if he travels with that rocker, Paul thought as headed toward the clubhouse.

When the Old Pro saw Paul, he smiled and said, "Put down those clubs—we're not getting to those quite yet. Come here and sit down, son."

"I thought we were going to work on my golf game and life," said Paul.

"We are," smiled the Old Pro. "But you will find you don't always have to hit balls to learn about golf."

As Paul sat down, the Old Pro turned to him and said, "Let me get right to the point, son. Why do you play golf?"

"That's a good question," said Paul. "I guess I play to have fun. By the way, you can call me Paul."

"Okay, Paul. Did you have fun yesterday?"

"Come to think of it, I didn't," said Paul.

"Why not?" asked the Old Pro.

"I was playing badly and when I don't do well, I don't have fun."

"Do you see why I asked you that question? If fun is a reason you play golf, then every golf game should be fun. I have never met a golf course or a golf game I didn't like. For me the worst a golf game can be is fabulous," said the Old Pro with a smile. "That's why I miss playing now."

"But haven't you had some bad days on the course?"

"Sure I have," said the Old Pro, "but I never thought that who I was on any given day depended on my score. I learned from bad days and laughed at bad days, but I never got down on myself because of a bad day."

"Interesting," said Paul. "I can't say that's been true for me."

"Is there any other reason you play golf?"

"I think the camaraderie and friendship is important," said Paul.

"What do you know about the three other guys you played with yesterday?"

"What do you mean?"

"Do you know anything about their lives, about their families, about their interests?"

"I don't."

"Why not?"

"I guess I was focusing too much on myself."

"Fine," said the Old Pro. "So if relationships are important to you, then you have to reach out to other people, don't you?"

Paul smiled. "You're really tough, aren't you? So I said I wanted to have fun and I wanted to have some good camaraderie, but I didn't have either of those yesterday. I guess I'm not walking my talk, am I?"

"Evidence is mounting up," said the Old Pro with a smile. "Is there any other reason you like to play golf?"

"This will probably get me in trouble too," said Paul. "I love the beauty of a golf course. Without golf courses, most of our cities would be cement."

"Tell me about the course you played yesterday. What kinds of trees dominated the landscape? What kinds of birds did you see?"

"You got me again," said Paul. "I didn't notice much about anything. I was so into myself."

"What do you think got in the way of your having fun, experiencing good camaraderie, and enjoying the beauty of the surroundings?" asked the Old Pro.

"Well," said Paul, "to be honest, I was so upset about how poorly I was playing in front of Davis Love and my teammates that I was too stressed-out to enjoy myself, my playing partners, or the course."

"There is no doubt in my mind," said the Old Pro, "that you have good intentions about those parts of golf, but I'm afraid you just turned golf into an achievement game."

"What's wrong with wanting to perform well and trying to be the best?"

"Before I answer that question, let me ask you another question," said the Old Pro. "What scoring system do you use to measure success in your life and when you play golf?"

"Here we go," said Paul. "I have a feeling this is probably why Davis suggested I meet with you."

"From what you told me yesterday I think you are probably right," said the Old Pro with a smile. "But seriously, where do your positive feelings about yourself come from?"

"Fortunately or unfortunately, I think they come from my performance and the opinion of others," said Paul. "If I perform well at work or I play well on the golf course and people respect me and appreciate what I do, I feel good about myself."

"That's interesting," said the Old Pro. "Let me ask you a couple of follow-up questions: Is your performance always good at work and on the golf course?"

"Of course not," said Paul. "I have my good days and my bad days like everyone else. Yesterday was a very bad day."

"So, if like everyone else you have a bad day once in a while, or even a bad month or quarter, it's also likely that your sense of self-worth is just as regularly at risk." The Old Pro's eyes twinkled.

"That's true," replied Paul. "It's hard to feel like a winner when the scorecard says something different."

"How has that been working for you — tying your feelings about yourself to the opinions of others?" inquired the Old Pro. "Can you always count on pleasing others? Can you always rely on their support?"

"No," Paul admitted. "I learned early in life that no matter how hard I tried, I couldn't find a father figure — an adult I could count on for approval and support — not my father and not my coach. This might sound funny, or just pathetic, but I guess I'm still looking. That's why I wanted to make a good impression on Davis — but my performance let me down."

"Given what you've said, don't you think you've placed your feelings of self-worth on shaky ground?" said the Old Pro.

"I guess you're right," said Paul.

"That's a tough way to live," said the Old Pro.

"Do you have any suggestions?"

"Absolutely," said the Old Pro. "I believe if you want to be good at golf and life, you have to stop putting your self-worth up for grabs based on your performance or the opinions of others. You have to approach life and golf from the point of view that your value and self-worth are secure beyond the ups and downs of how well you might be scoring at the moment or how much applause or criticism you are hearing from the crowd. I see so many people who beat themselves up while they play golf, and I am sure that they beat themselves up when they play life. Most of us don't need anyone else criticizing us, because we do enough of it on our own. So before I help anyone, I want to make sure they know that their golf game is not their score, and their life is not their performance plus the opinion of others."

"I think I see where you're going," Paul replied. "You're suggesting that if my main intention for playing golf is to win or to impress others, it will make it impossible for me to succeed in enjoying other aspects of the game. But if I focus on having fun, getting to know my playing partners, and enjoying the beauty of the environment, I'll probably relax and play better golf."

"You've got it," said the Old Pro with a smile.

"Thanks," said Paul smiling back. "You're suggesting that my present scoring system puts my sense of self-worth up for grabs on every shot. You're also saying that I'm missing the reasons I said I have for playing the game in the first place."

"Don't I have living evidence sitting right next to me?"

said the Old Pro, chuckling.

"I'm afraid you do," said Paul. "Is there any way out of this?"

"There are two ways," said the Old Pro. "The first is to play golf just to have fun, enjoy the people you play with, and appreciate the beauty around you. That's how I got my wife interested in golf."

"If I'd tried that," said Paul with an ironic smile, "my marriage probably would have ended sooner."

"Not if you taught your wife that there are only three rules to playing golf," said the Old Pro. "The first is not to hurt anybody with your club or your ball. The second is not to hold anyone up — "

"That really drives me crazy!" Paul blurted.

"I agree," said the Old Pro. "That's why one of the first things I taught my wife to do was to bend down, pick up her ball, put it in her pocket, and go to the next hole. It doesn't make any sense to see someone shaking over a three-foot putt for an eight or nine."

"I agree," said Paul. "What's the third rule?"

"Don't ruin the environment," said the Old Pro. "Replace your divots. Don't drive a golf cart near a green or drag a pull cart onto the green."

"I like those rules," said Paul.

"They're the best," said the Old Pro, "because as long as you follow them, you can do anything you want. If you want to kick the ball, then kick it. If you want to throw the ball, then throw it. You rented the hole. Just don't hurt anyone, hold people up, or ruin the environment."

"That's wild," said Paul. "I can't see myself playing like that."

"I played that way many times when I was young," said the Old Pro. "I'll never forget playing with three corporate presidents from the Northeast. They came to Florida for a conference early in the spring when it was still cold up north. They asked if I would play with them. I said sure, but realizing that none of them had played golf since the end of October, I suggested we play a special game. Everyone was allowed one throw a hole."

"One throw a hole!" shouted Paul.

"That's exactly how they reacted," said the Old Pro. "When I insisted, they had trouble doing it the first few holes. But then they really got into it. They had more fun deciding whether they would use their throw on the green, out of a sand trap, or out of the trees. At the end of the round, they said they had never had a better time."

"Wow," said Paul. "What's the second way to make sure your self-worth isn't up for grabs all the time?"

"The second way is to discover and accept the fact that your self-worth is already secure. It is not subject to how well you do or what people think of you," replied the Old Pro.

"Tell me more," said Paul.

"Let me ask you a personal question, Paul. Do you believe in God?"

"I hope you're not going to get religious on me," said Paul. "I'm not religious at all."

"You can relax," said the Old Pro. "I'm not talking about religion. I'm talking about God. Let me repeat my question. Do you believe in God?"

"I haven't given it much thought, but I guess so."

"I hope so," said the Old Pro. "In my opinion, not believing in God makes about as much sense as saying the unabridged dictionary is a result of an explosion in a print shop."

"Okay," said Paul. "But I don't see how what I believe or don't believe about God has any relevance to my golf game or my self-worth."

"This may be new thinking for you, Paul, but let me tell you what I have come to believe over the past fifty years." The Old Pro turned to face him. "See, the God I worship is a loving God. I don't think he made any junk, which means I think he unconditionally loves me and you. As a result, I can't perform well enough, play well enough, or do anything well enough to change the love and value God has already placed on my life—I have all the love I need. My value in God's eyes is never up for grabs.

"Now, that doesn't mean I don't make mistakes, or that I don't have areas I need to improve. But my self-worth is rock-solid in God's love. I pay attention to what I do and try to correct my mistakes every day and change my behavior, but I don't beat myself up. I know I am forgiven and accepted."

Paul shifted his weight uncomfortably. "With all due respect, that sounds great if it works for you, but I'm not ready to accept what you are saying without a lot of thought."

"Take your time," said the Old Pro. "God isn't in a hurry and neither am I. Just remember that he is only one conversation away."

"Not to change the subject too quickly," said Paul, pausing, "but when am I going to have my first *golf lesson*?"

"You just had it!" said the Old Pro, his eyes twinkling again. "Think about what we have talked about and call me the next time you are down here so that we can get together again."

When Paul saw the Old Pro stand up and extend his hand, he realized the lesson was over.

As Paul drove away from the Muni, his mind was working overtime. The more he thought about the short exchange he'd had with the Old Pro, the more he realized he had gotten a great lesson — one that was hard for an achievement-motivated guy like him to hear. But it was a lesson he'd needed to hear.

On the flight back to Atlanta Paul thought to himself, *It's good I'm not planning on giving up my day job for golf. If I were trying to make a living as a golf pro, my performance probably would be important.*

Then again, the Old Pro had told him that if you evaluate yourself every day by your performance, even if you were a golf pro, you'd probably never become a great player. "You have to have a solid self-worth to endure the ups and downs of the game," he'd said.

Paul realized that even Ben Hogan, Arnold Palmer, Jack Nicklaus, and all the greats in the game had some tough times and disappointments. In fact, Paul remembered reading about how Hogan fought his wild hook for years but stayed with it until he finally could put his game in perspective.

On his flight back to Atlanta later that afternoon, Paul looked out the window and reflected on his day. He pulled his journal from his carry-on and recorded his insights.

•   •   •

Solid Shots

I had my first meeting with the Old Pro, Willie Dunn, today. It wasn't anything like I had expected. But then again, I had no idea what to expect. I did think he would at least watch me swing a club. Oh well, I did well not to say anything about that. I'm sure he'll watch me hit the ball next time.

I learned some interesting lessons from Will. Not sure I buy it all, but here it is:

- If my scoring system for playing golf is all about winning and the opinion of others, I will miss out on what the game is all about: having fun, building relationships, and enjoying the environment.

- My self-worth is not a product of my performance plus the opinion of others. (That would be nice.)
- There are only three rules for golf: don't hurt anyone, don't hold anyone up, and don't harm the environment. Once you know these rules you have rented the hole. (I really like this one.)
- God did not make junk. I am unconditionally loved.
- I am valuable even though there are parts of my life that could be improved.
- God is only one conversation away. (No idea what this one means!)

Mulligans

I didn't really need any today. The Old Pro kept me off the course so I stayed out of the hazards.

To be honest, I could use some mulligans to help me get over all the times I played just to impress others rather than to have fun, enjoy others playing with me, and appreciate the beauty of the environment.

CHAPTER 7

BACK TO REALITY

ALL POSITIVE THINKING went out the window the next morning when Paul's alarm went off. He leapt out of bed and hit the road running. He tried to eat while he was washing. He jumped into his car and immediately was on his cell phone. His three-day journey to Asheville had taken its toll: his email was jammed, his voice mail was full, his in-basket was overflowing, and everyone wanted to see him.

A hectic morning was followed by a lunch meeting, a full afternoon, and then a dinner meeting. By the time he got home at 9:30, he was so exhausted he did not even take his clothes off. He just flopped onto the bed and went instantly to sleep.

When the alarm went off the next morning, Paul was off and running again. This day looked to be as hectic as the last. Then a quote in a magazine article on time management that he was reading pulled him up short. It was by the movie star Lily Tomlin: "The problem with being in a rat race is that even if you win the race, you are still a rat."

Suddenly Paul realized his life was a rat race for results. He was addicted to making things happen and generating pay-off on the bottom line. Remembering the Old Pro's statement that life "was all about relationships," he briefly wondered what this drive for success was doing to his relationships. He already knew what it had done to his relationship with his son Jake. He hadn't seen him in two years. Every time they planned to get together something came up. It cut him to the quick when he last spoke to his son on the phone and Jake said, "Dad, why don't you just admit that your life doesn't have room for a son? Don't call me anymore and tell me you are coming to see me. If you just show up sometime, I'll believe it."

All this made Paul think about the Old Pro. He needed to see him again more than ever. Early the next morning, Paul checked with his secretary to see if he had some free time in his schedule. Paul found himself on the short flight from Atlanta to Asheville ten days later.

•　　•　　•

Solid Shots

Maybe I should add a heading called "Intentions." I sure intended to be positive with people and make relationships a priority, but I did not make a solid relational shot all day! I got a good deal behind on some business when I stayed over to meet with the Old Pro. I almost killed myself, but I answered all my past emails, returned all my voicemail messages, approved or rerouted all my in-basket items, and at least contacted or left a message with everyone who wanted to see me. I tried to get caught up. I guess that's worth something.

Mulligans

I was a little testy with my secretary right before lunch. Okay, I was flat out rude and sharp with her. I guess my hunger was getting to me. Then, I got short and impatient with the valet kid when he brought me the wrong car. I mean, how many silver BMWs have "TAKE IT" on the license plate? If relationships are as important as the Old Pro says, I suspect I have a lot to learn about this part of my life.

I thought about Jake and felt the same pit in my stomach that I have felt for a couple of years. Maybe I should try to connect with him.

I'm not sure I like keeping a journal, but I'm not about to stop now. I may be a lot of things, but a quitter is not one of them!

CHAPTER 8

PREPARING TO PLAY

PAUL WAS EXCITED about his second lesson with the Old Pro. As he pulled up to the Muni, he could see Will on the putting green with a group of young kids. He could not tell if the Old Pro was giving a lesson or just playing a game with them. Paul sat in his car for a moment and soaked in the blue sky, the green grass, and the picture in front of him. *This could be a Norman Rockwell painting called Old Will Dunn and the kids on the green*, Paul thought.

Paul decided to leave his clubs in the car because he wasn't sure if he'd ever get to hit any balls. But the more he thought about his last visit, the less he cared.

As he got out of the car and walked toward the empty rocking chair on the clubhouse porch, Paul heard the Old Pro say, "Okay kids, that's it for now." They let out a collective groan of disappointment and spontaneously mobbed the Old Pro with a group hug. For a moment Paul thought they would knock the old man over, but Will just laughed and patted the kids on their heads as he sent them off.

Once he was seated in his rocker, the Old Pro waggled his putter and said to Paul, "I can't tell you how much I love spending time with those kids."

"It shows."

"How are you doing, Paul?" said the Old Pro with a welcoming smile. "Are you ready for your next lesson?"

"Sure am. Are we going to do it here or out on the range?"

"Sit down," said the Old Pro. "Let's talk first and then I'll have a better idea of what would be most helpful. Tell me all! What's been happening with you since we last talked?"

"Well," said Paul with a sigh, "I was excited when I left here last time. You really made me look at golf and my life with a different set of glasses. But before a blink of the eye, I was back in the rat race. When the alarm went off every day, I jumped out of bed and hit the road running."

"What an unfortunate term," the Old Pro muttered to himself.

"What term?"

"Alarm clock," started the Old Pro. "Why don't they call it the 'opportunity' clock or the 'it's going to be a great day' clock?"

"Good point," said Paul with a laugh. "Talk about programming your mind in a negative way."

"The problem," the Old Pro began, "is that we all have two selves: an inner self that is thoughtful, reflective, and a good listener; and an outer, task-oriented self that is focused on achieving and getting things done. The outer self is too busy to learn. And which of these two selves do you think wakes up quicker in the morning?"

"That's easy," said Paul. "It's our task-oriented self. When we jump out of bed after shutting off the alarm, our attention turns to all the things we have to do that day."

"Exactly," said the Old Pro. "As a result, few people ever wake up their inner selves. We don't even do it on vacation. We race around from one activity to another and then come home exhausted."

"What's the answer?" wondered Paul.

"The way to avoid the rat race," said the Old Pro, "is to honor your inner self by seeking quiet and solitude."

"How can you find time for solitude?" asked Paul.

"I recommend you enter your day more slowly," said the Old Pro.

"Does that have anything to do with my golf game?" asked Paul.

"It sure does," said the Old Pro. "Entering your day slowly prepares you to be the best you can be during that day. What do you do to prepare yourself to play golf?

"I'm always amazed at the number of golfers who have hardly any time to warm up mentally or physically before starting a round of golf. Sometimes you see them tying their shoes on the first tee. I have the feeling that you might fall into that category."

"Guilty as charged," said Paul sheepishly. "The day I played with Davis Love, I was racing there just to make our tee-off time. I got there with a few minutes to spare, ran to the practice tee to beat a few balls, and raced back to the first tee."

"I anticipated as much," said the Old Pro with a nod. "In an ideal world it would be best to head out to the golf course at a leisurely pace, arriving about an hour before you are scheduled to play. Remember: On the way to the course, you need some way to transition from what you have been doing to the task at hand—playing and enjoying a round of golf."

"How did you do that when you were playing a lot?" asked Paul.

"If you noticed, on your way to the Muni, you passed through beautiful, remote countryside."

"To be honest with you I barely noticed," Paul admitted. "I was thinking about a problem I have at work."

"Case closed," said the Old Pro with a smile. "Whenever I headed out here to play golf I would tune into some soothing music on my radio and begin to soak in the beauty of the surroundings. By the time I arrived at the course I was mellow and relaxed—a perfect way to set the stage for an enjoyable round of golf. I did the same thing today so I could be focused on helping you and enjoying our time together."

"It would be difficult for me to quiet my mind the way you do," said Paul. "But I can see the power in it. Suppose I developed a relaxing routine coming to the course and I arrived forty-five minutes to an hour before I was scheduled to play. What should I do when I arrive?"

"First, sit in your car, quiet yourself, and think about any concerns you have that might get in your way of playing well and enjoying the great game of golf. Then lay each of those concerns down."

"Just get them out of my mind," said Paul.

"You got it," said the Old Pro. "Then visualize yourself later that day, sitting with the people you played with, laughing and feeling great because you had fun, enjoyed their company, soaked in the beauty around you, and played well. Be pleased with your performance. Then head to the locker room, change your shoes, and get ready to play."

"And then I go to the range and start hitting balls?"

"Not right away — relax," said the Old Pro in a gentle, caring way.

"I'll be so relaxed I'll be like a wet noodle," said Paul with a laugh, "and I won't be able to hit the ball."

"Yes, you will," said the Old Pro. "But first, before you head out to the range, I recommend doing some stretching exercises. This gets you loosened up before hitting any balls."

"I went to a golf school once," said Paul, "and they gave me a little booklet that had the stretches they taught us.

But, as you can imagine, I never got to do them because usually I only had time to hit a few balls before teeing off. If the choice is between stretching or hitting a few balls, I'll smack the white pill anytime."

"Most people make the same choice," said the Old Pro. "But sometimes with a good stretching routine, you don't even have to hit any balls."

"Really?"

"Really!" he said. "In Scotland, where the game of golf originated, there are few driving ranges. So you stretch and then begin your round. I've played over there many times, and it doesn't seem to hurt me or anybody else if we don't hit any balls ahead of time."

"So I shouldn't hit any practice balls?" asked Paul.

"I didn't say that," said the Old Pro. "If you do hit balls, which is by no means a bad idea, your intent should be to loosen up, not to work on swing mechanics. Right before a round is not the time to revamp your swing. You have to go with what you brought to the dance.

"Too many golfers are playing 'golf swing' on the course," continued the Old Pro, "including some of the top pros. If something goes wrong and they're hooking or slicing the ball, they try to correct it in the middle of the round. Things usually go from bad to worse."

"What do you recommend?"

"Correct the problem on the practice tee after the round or schedule a lesson with your local pro. When you are on the course, just play golf. See how few strokes you can take, regardless of whether you're hitting the ball straight, crooked, or what have you. Whatever it takes for you to get the ball into the cup. And whatever you do, don't watch other amateurs swing. Play your own game. You don't want a lot of negative images filling your mind."

"I noticed that Davis Love didn't pay much attention to my swing the other day at the Pro-Am," said Paul.

"That's because he's learned the secret of not playing 'golf swing,'" said the Old Pro.

"I don't imagine people who play 'golf swing' on the course are much fun to be around," said Paul with a laugh. "I play it all the time on the course. That's what destroyed my game in the Pro-Am with Love. When I work on my swing during a round, all the other purposes for playing golf go out the window except focusing on my score."

"Talking about that," said the Old Pro, "while you are getting into the rhythm of the game on the range, it might be a good time to review why you play golf. Is it for fun, for camaraderie, for beauty, or for the competition? Make sure you don't forget about your purpose. No matter what happens on the course, you need to keep your reasons for playing golf paramount. Otherwise, as you have indicated, you may let your results determine whether you enjoy the round or not."

"I feel a bit like I'm in the third grade," said Paul. "You have made that point over and over and over again."

"That's because I want you to get it right — right — right!" said the Old Pro with a wide smile. "Why don't you get your clubs and I'll meet you by the practice green. You can hit a few chips and putts and then go to the range and slowly move from your wedge up to your driver."

"That's an interesting approach," said Paul. "I usually finish my practicing with a few chips and putts."

"Most people do," said the Old Pro. "But I think it is good to complete your loosening up routine with your driver, or whatever you hit off the tee, because that will be the first club you use on the course."

"Does that mean we're going to get on the course?" Paul asked hopefully.

"Yes," said the Old Pro. "I'll ride around with you while you play nine holes."

Paul raced to the car, grabbed his clubs, and met the Old Pro at the putting green. After a few putts and chips he headed to the driving range and followed the Old Pro's sequence of clubs, ending with his driver.

CHAPTER 9

SETTING YOUR OWN PAR

"SIT DOWN ON THE CART," instructed the Old Pro. When Paul sat down, the Old Pro showed him the scorecard and said, "Just so you don't get the idea that I don't think your score is important, now that you're loosened up, let's look at the scorecard from the course and begin to set your own par."

"My own par?" repeated Paul.

"Yes," said the Old Pro. "It does not make sense for you to play against the course par of seventy-two unless you are a pro. As a result, I've developed a goal-setting system designed to help people compete against their own par. Here's how it works:

"It starts with some brutal honesty," said the Old Pro. "The par for this first nine is thirty-six, and I would say that this front nine is moderately difficult. What did you say your handicap was?"

"I don't think I did," said Paul. "But I am a twelve. That's a little low, though, for how I've been playing lately."

"I've heard that before," said the Old Pro with a chuckle. "Sounds like you're negotiating a bet. Unfortunately, I won't be playing. Now, given how you're feeling after loosening up—and add to that the facts that you don't feel you've been playing as well as you should lately and you've never played this course before—what score would you be pleased to report if we were sitting in the clubhouse having an ice-cold glass of sweet tea after nine holes?"

Paul looked over the card. "I think I'd feel good if I shot forty-four."

"In terms of the course par, then, *your* par for this nine would be eight bogies and one par, but you can set up your own par any way you want."

"What do you mean?"

"Suppose you tend to start slow and finish strong," said the Old Pro. "You might want to set your par on the first hole, which is a par four, at six. Now, if you get a five on the first hole when your par was six, it is a psychological lift to be able to go to the second tee one under par rather than one over."

"That could be exciting," said Paul. "So I can set par for myself on any given hole at any amount as long as my total adds up to my hoped-for goal of forty-four."

"You've got it!" said the Old Pro. "Suppose you start to set eighty-nine as your goal for eighteen holes. Once you start to shoot consistently below that goal, you could lower your goal to eighty-seven and begin to stretch yourself again. With this system you are being specific and giving yourself a goal to shoot at, not only for the entire round but also for each hole—a goal that might be more realistic than the course-designated par for professionals."

"The system sounds good to me," said Paul as he wrote down a six for the par-four first hole, a five for the rest of the par fours, a six for the two par fives, and two threes for the par threes. That gave him a score of forty-four. "I think I'm ready to go," said Paul.

"Let's do it," said the Old Pro as he drove the golf cart to the first tee.

On the first hole, a par four up the hill, Paul had a good drive, but his second shot landed in a sand trap. His first two sand shots caught the lip of the trap and rolled back into the bunker. His third shot from the trap finally landed on the green and he two-putted for a seven. A frustrated Paul walked back to the golf cart and slammed his sand wedge into his bag. When he sat down he started to write seven on his scorecard. The Old Pro intervened.

"With this scoring system, you don't write down your actual score, only how many shots you were under or over your par," said the Old Pro. "So write down for the first hole a plus one. That means for *your* par you had a bogey."

"So because I set my par at six, and got a seven, I have a bogey rather than a triple bogey? That's great!"

"Doesn't that make you feel better?" said the Old Pro with a laugh.

"I know what you're getting at," said Paul. "I'll just have to get that seven out of my head." On the next hole, a long par five, Paul's par was six. Again his drive was good but his second shot landed in the rough and he had to chop it out with a wedge. His fourth shot went flying over the green and Paul shouted, "Jesus Christ!" as he slammed his club into the ground. When he regained his composure, he chipped back onto the putting surface within five feet but missed the putt for another seven.

"Two thoughts on that hole," said the Old Pro with a smile. "First of all, if you're going to bring up Jesus at all, I find it's always better to talk to him before you hit your shot rather than after it. He could be more helpful then."

Paul said with a sheepish look, "What's your second thought?"

"That's another plus-one bogey," said the Old Pro with a twinkle in his eye.

"So I am two over par for the first two holes. I guess it's a lot better than being five over."

"It sure is," said the Old Pro. "Let's see how you do on the next hole, a short par four where your par is five."

Paul hit another good drive down the middle of the fairway. His eight iron hit the green and rolled ten feet from the cup. As he got back in the golf cart to drive to the green, he smiled and said, "I'm putting for an eagle three."

"You're starting to get it," said the Old Pro.

Paul missed the putt but got to write down a minus one birdie on the scorecard. He captured his par three on the next hole and went to the fifth tee one over par. The fifth hole was a four-hundred-and-forty-yard par four. Paul hit a good drive but still had over two hundred yards uphill to the green.

"What club would you use if you were trying to hit it onto the green from here?" asked the Old Pro.

"I'd hit my three wood," said Paul.

"What's the probability that you could hit a three wood two hundred yards up the hill to this green?"

"Probably not very high," said Paul.

"Tell me something," said the Old Pro. "If you had a choice, would you rather be hitting a thirty-yard half wedge or a full ninety-yard wedge?"

"To be honest with you," said Paul, "I'd rather have a ninety-yard shot."

"Since the probability is not high that you can hit the green with your three wood, why risk getting into trouble in a trap or rough or having one of those difficult half-wedge shots? Take out your pitching wedge and hit a shot about a hundred and ten yards down the middle to that ninety-yard range," said the Old Pro.

"If I did that with my cronies at my club," said Paul, "they would laugh at me."

"Remember what you learned last time," said the Old Pro. "Your self-worth is not a function of the opinions of others. If you would rather hit a full wedge than a half wedge, then why not play your second shot to where you could hit that kind of shot, especially since this is a par five for you?"

"There's more to this scoring system than meets the eye," said Paul.

"Absolutely!" said the Old Pro. "It's a strategy for setting realistic goals, not only for every hole and every round, but also for every shot."

Paul took out his pitching wedge and hit it beautifully to where he was able to hit a full wedge to the green. Having a shot where he felt confident, Paul relaxed and hit a good shot. His ball landed five feet from the pin and this time his putt went right into the center of the cup. Paul let out a scream. "Another birdie! I'm back to even par!"

"Good going," the Old Pro shouted back.

Paul scored *his par* on the next two holes, including a beautiful three from the sand trap on the par-three seventh hole. The eighth hole was a dogleg left par five with a brook in front of the green. Paul hit two good shots, putting himself in a good position for a full wedge to the green. When his third shot landed on the green and he two-putted, Paul was thrilled to write a minus one on the card for a birdie five on what was a par-six hole for him.

He was now one under par for the round. When he got *his* par five on the tough par-four ninth hole, Paul was pleased to write down a forty-three for his score on the nine holes.

CHAPTER 10

ENTERING YOUR DAY SLOWLY

SITTING IN THE CLUBHOUSE sipping an iced tea, Paul smiled and said, "Any other day if I started off with two sevens, I would have been in the tank and never rallied. Translating those scores into two plus-one bogies and not writing a seven down on the card really helped. Your scoring system, plus the suggestions for preparing to play golf, should improve my game. But what about my life?"

"As I recommended earlier, you should enter your day more slowly," with a smile the Old Pro.

"Preparing for a golf game is one thing, but I'm not sure I can fit anything more into my schedule," said Paul with a laugh.

"I know the feeling," said the Old Pro, "but it takes discipline. Let me share what has worked for me. I must admit I don't do what I'll describe every day. It's stupid but true. It's called free will in action. My hunch is that all of us have the same problem — we know we need to spend more time in quiet reflection, but we let other things crowd that time. Maybe that is why mornings work best for me.

"When I am being really good to myself, I try to make quiet time the first priority of the day before anything else — like a phone call or time with a new friend like you — has a chance to interfere."

"So mornings are best?" asked Paul.

"That's what works for me," said the Old Pro. "For example, research shows that morning exercisers seem to maintain a regular exercise program longer than afternoon and evening exercisers."

"Why?"

"Because things come up later in the day that interfere with good intentions," said the Old Pro. "If you take care of your inner self when you get up in the morning, the rest of the day never seems quite as hectic."

"So tell me what you do."

"When my day starts off well," began the Old Pro, "one of the first things I do is sit quietly and relax. Then I begin doing some stretching to help loosen up this old body. I mention stretching because while I am trying to wake up my body, it's a perfect time to talk to the Good Lord. He's my friend and he wants to hear from me."

"So you pray?" asked Paul, surprised.

"Yes I do," the Old Pro asserted. "But I shy away from using that term when talking to people about my time with the Lord. When you mention prayer, people want to know how to do it. Then talking to the Good Lord becomes more about a technique than a conversation with a good friend."

"So that's what you meant when you said God was just one conversation away."

"Exactly," said the Old Pro with a smile. "It's so easy to think of prayer as an event or obligation rather than as a way of life. It's simply talking to a friend along the course of your day from the start to the finish."

"And, you think of God as your friend?" asked Paul.

"Absolutely!" said the Old Pro. "I think of him as my best friend." He paused. "Do you ever talk to God?"

"No ... Well, except when I'm worried about something. I'm embarrassed to say that the only time I talk to God is when I could use his help. I would imagine if I looked at him as a good friend the way you do, he would want to hear from me more often and not just when I am in trouble."

"That's true," said the Old Pro, "I know he is glad to hear from you anytime. The Good Book says we are to talk to our friend all the time. That's why he made us, to walk along with him. Because he loves us, it has always been his plan that we have a close relationship with him. To prove that point, let me ask you about your son. You told me you had a son the last time we met, but we never talked much about him. How old is he?"

Feeling ashamed about the lack of contact with his son, Paul looked down and mumbled, "He's twenty-two. We don't have much contact anymore."

"Has that always been the case?" asked the Old Pro.

"Yes," Paul admitted. "I was never there for him. And since the divorce I've just been too busy. Just like my father, Jake started drinking. Then five years ago he was driving home from a party drunk and caused a serious car accident—one of his friends was critically injured. It was painful for me to see my son go through that. I wanted to help but didn't know how to reach out."

"I'll bet if your son called you and said he was in trouble, you would forget all that, listen, and still try to help."

"Despite our differences in the past, I still love him. I am sure I would," Paul said.

"God's the same way," said the Old Pro. "He's always available when you need him no matter what you have done or how long it has been since your last conversation. But I'll have to admit: Your relationship with God gets better and more intimate when talking things over with him is your first response rather than your last resort."

"If I decided to talk with God more frequently," said Paul, "I wouldn't know what to say or do."

"Most people worry too much about that," said the Old Pro. "Now I know you said earlier that you could never count on your father. But suppose you could, and in your mind he was the greatest, most loving father anyone could ever have. That's who your Heavenly Father is. So just talk to him like he is your best friend."

"What do I talk to him about?"

"Well, if you can't think of anything else—tell him how great he is!" said the Old Pro with a smile. "Tell him about the problems or concerns you have. You might want to admit any mistakes you've made and tell him you're sorry. Thank him for all he has done for you. Then ask him for what you need. Just start talking with him on a regular basis and you'll figure it out."

"That sounds simple enough," said Paul.

"It is," said the Old Pro. "Let me tell you another thing I do during my quiet time. I always spend a few moments in silence, listening, in case the good Lord wants to say something to me."

"You know, I've heard people say, 'God told me,' and I always wondered what they were talking about. They give the impression that God speaks to them directly in a clear, loud voice. I certainly have never heard God speak to me," said Paul.

"Neither have I," said the Old Pro, "not with my ears. Yet, I'm convinced I have heard from God. In trying to figure out how he communicates with me, I asked myself, *When do I do the best thinking? When do I think most clearly: is it in the shower? Taking a walk? Reading?* I realized that I think most clearly when I am interacting with people the Lord puts in my path. If all truth and knowledge comes from God, then I figure that's when he is talking to me. So, whenever I meet an interesting person like you, I always think to myself, *God, what do you want me to learn?* When I am quiet before him and ask a question like that, my thoughts are directed to the things he wants me to think about. That's when it is particularly important for me to listen."

"I think most clearly when I am reading," said Paul. "Do you think that's the way God talks to me?"

"Could be. He has used both the written and spoken word to communicate with his children," said the Old Pro. "I think God talks to us all in special and unique ways. But if you're looking for a burning bush, that's already taken."

Not understanding the burning bush reference, Paul carried on: "How else does God speak to you?" he asked.

"Through his love letter to me," said the Old Pro with a smile. "It's best known as the Bible," he continued.

"I once heard someone say that the Bible stands for **B**asic **I**nstruction **B**efore **L**eaving **E**arth," said Paul. "What do you think of that?"

The Old Pro laughed out loud. "I like it! That's a humorous way to remember that the Bible contains all kinds of good advice for the art of living and messages of love from the Father to his children. Remember, reading the Bible is more than a reading assignment; it's a way to get to know and understand God and how he wants you to live in relation to him and to other people. For example I have a plaque next to my bed with Psalm 118:24 on it. When I read, 'This is the day the Lord has made; let us rejoice and be glad in it,' it starts my day off right."

"Over the years I've done a lot of inspirational reading," said Paul. "But to be honest with you, I really haven't spent much time reading the Bible. Every time I tried, I would get bogged down in some list of details that just didn't make any sense."

"You ought to try the Good Book again, Paul, if you want to learn how to play the **G**ame **O**f **L**ife **F**irst, the way the designer of the course meant it to be played," said the Old Pro with a smile. "It's been a best seller for a long time. I seldom come away from reading the Bible without learning some important new nugget of truth about my journey."

Changing topics, Paul said, "Is there anything else you do to enter your day slowly?"

"On an ideal day, when I finish stretching, talking and listening to God, and reading his Word, I do some aerobic exercise," said the Old Pro. "The Bible calls the body the temple of the Lord, and I need to be good to this old temple. So every morning I get my five iron for a walking stick and head out for a short walk with my dog. He loves it and so do I."

"What if it's raining?" asked Paul.

"I do it rain or shine," said the Old Pro. "I learned a long time ago there is no bad weather, only inappropriate clothing."

"That's a good one," Paul said with a smile.

"Besides," continued the Old Pro, "I found out there is a difference between interest and commitment."

"Tell me more," said Paul.

"When interested exercisers wake up in the morning and it's raining outside, they say to themselves, *I'll exercise tomorrow*. Committed people don't know about excuses; they only know about results. So if committed exercisers wake up and it is raining outside, they say to themselves *I think I'll exercise inside*, or *I'd better wear my rain gear*. People committed to doing something have a 'no matter what' philosophy."

"Interesting," mused Paul. "I'm a runner. I've entered a number of 10K races and have been thinking about preparing for a half-marathon."

"When you make exercise part of how you enter your day slowly, you have to be careful not to treat it as another achievement game. I think it's great that you compete in some 10Ks, but you might want to try something in the morning that helps to continue to awaken your inner self. A friend of mine was a morning jogger for more than twenty years. He is now more of a walker, but I love to be around him when people ask how far he walks every day. His reply is, 'I don't know.' They usually counter with, 'Well, how long do you walk each day?' Again my friend says, 'I don't know. My morning walk is not about getting anywhere. It's just a way I choose to enter my day.'"

"What a great approach to morning exercise," said Paul. "I can see what you're saying. The purpose of your morning exercise is to provide you with more inner peace. That's something I sure can work on."

"I end my morning time alone by sitting quietly again," said the Old Pro. "I put my hands on my knees and think about all the concerns I have about the day. As they come to mind, I just hand them off to the Lord.

"When I've laid down my last concern," continued the Old Pro, "I turn my hands upward in a receiving mode, signaling I'm ready to do his will as I walk through the day in the company of my *friend*. I imagine sitting here at night before I go to bed, feeling good about what we did together during the day and how I've behaved and interacted with others."

"I can understand why your routine for entering your day slowly takes discipline. There are a lot of components to it," said Paul.

"It does take discipline," said the Old Pro, "but I am positively addicted to it. When I skip a day, which I told you happens from time to time, I almost go through withdrawal symptoms, like people with negative addictions. My day does not seem to flow as well when I have not taken time to reflect and listen to the Good Lord. I read a wonderful quote recently: 'When fog settles in over a seaport, ships listen for the foghorn to know where the dangers are. The sound of the horn helps them stay on course.' We, too, need to listen, so that we don't stray off course."

"I get it," said Paul. "My old habit of charging hard through life leaves little time for reflection and listening to a voice much wiser than my own."

"You've got that right," said the Old Pro.

"I can't thank you enough," Paul said.

"The real way you can thank me," said the Old Pro, "is to put some of what you've learned today into practice. Why don't we get together again in about a month?"

"You're on," said Paul. "I'll check my schedule and give you a call when I get back to the office."

• • •

Solid Shots

Met again with the Old Pro and to my surprise I actually hit balls. Ironically, he made no comments about my swing. However, I did learn to set my own par. The whole idea seemed contrived and strange at first. But I gave it a try, had fun, and actually shot a solid forty-three on a tough nine I had never played.

The Old Pro gave me some tips to help me get out of the rat race, slow down, and reduce the number of mulligans I need both in GOLF and LIFE. I don't understand everything he talked about, but I listened and will try to use some of this advice in the coming days:

- The alarm clock could be called the "opportunity" or "have a great day" clock.
- I can enter my day slowly by sitting quietly, relaxing, stretching, having a conversation with the Good Lord (that's what prayer is all about), listening, reading the Bible (I'm skeptical on this one), and planning on having a great day.
- Remember that exercise is not an achievement game.
- I can visualize walking through a perfect day in the company of God as my best friend.

Mulligans

Thanks to my conversations with the Old Pro and learning about the importance of relationships, I am thinking more about my son than I have in a long time. If there is anyone I wish I could have a mulligan with, it would be Jake (and I suppose his mom). I feel like I don't deserve another chance, but it doesn't hurt to hope.

I'm not sure what I think about all the "Good Book," "Good Lord," and "Listening to God" stuff. But I am sure that I move too fast. I don't ever seem to slow down. I think I might need a mulligan here. I need to learn how to slow down, on the golf course and in life. Everything is a race and a competition in my mind. I want to dial it back a bit, and I think some of the Old Pro's ideas just might help get me on the right track. I'm going to do a few experiments with these ideas and see if they lead to some mulligans in my life.

CHAPTER 11

STUMBLING THE MUMBLE

ON THE FLIGHT BACK to Atlanta Paul couldn't get over how much he had learned from the Old Pro. He thought about the round of golf he had scheduled for the coming Saturday and mapped out a strategy for implementing some of the golf lessons he had learned.

Paul thought, *On the way to the course I need a way to transition—ease into my golf game. I will arrive forty-five minutes early and do the following:*

- Quiet myself and lay down my concerns.
- Tip the kid who helps with my clubs and try to smile at him and act appreciative.
- Visualize feeling good at the end of the round because I had fun, enjoyed people, noticed the environment, and played well.

- Take time to stretch.
- Hit some balls to loosen up, starting with putting and chipping and gradually working down to my driver.
- Set my own par for each hole that adds up to my hoped-for score for the day.
- Focus on playing golf, not "golf swing" — go with what I brought to the party.
- Do my best to play to my own par.

As Paul reflected on his plan, his biggest concern was whether or not he could put into practice all that he'd learned. "Only time will tell," he mumbled aloud.

When Paul got home, he successfully entered his day slowly for the first three days. But then a business crisis hit the fan and he was off and running again.

On Saturday he had a scheduled tee-off time at ten o'clock. He fully intended to take a relaxing ride through the countryside on the way to the course and implement the plan he had laid out to start slowly.

At eight o'clock that morning Paul's phone rang and his plans went out the window. The call was from his son, Jake, who was very upset. He had been laid off from his job at a manufacturing company where he had worked since graduating from college. He was still paying off his college loans and some bad credit card debts and didn't know what to do, so he was calling to see if he could come live with Paul until he got his head above water.

Paul couldn't believe it. *The Old Pro was prophetic*, he thought. He could hear him say again, "I bet if your son called you and said he was in trouble, you would listen and try to help." *Why did I say "I sure would"?* Paul chastised himself. *This really is inconvenient*, he thought. "Is there any other alternative?" Paul heard himself say.

"Mom is still all tied up with taking care of Nana since her stroke last year, so I have no place else to turn."

The old last resort, thought Paul. Then, softening, he said, "When do you want to come?"

"Would tomorrow be all right?"

You have got to be kidding me! thought Paul. All of a sudden, he imagined the Old Pro standing by his side saying, *It's okay, you can handle it. Your son needs you. Don't miss this opportunity.* With this in mind, he replied, "Let's make it work. I'll have my travel agent make a flight reservation for you from New York to Atlanta."

After a call to his travel agent, Paul decided to keep his golf date. He arrived at the course with ten minutes to spare. *Not the best way to start a golf game*, he thought to himself with a laugh. *I guess laughter is better than tears.* Paul hit a few chip shots and putts; then tried to do some loosening-up exercises. When he went to the first tee he was hardly relaxed. He hit his opening drive out of bounds. As he always did, he refused to take a mulligan when it was offered and took the prescribed one-shot penalty, playing his third shot off the tee. His round went downhill from there.

In the weeks that followed, the strain of getting reconnected with his son and his career problems, plus one crisis after another at work, made it difficult for Paul to walk the talk and put into practice what the Old Pro had taught him. On top of that his relationship with his girlfriend, Carla, went south. The intrusion of his son into their relationship and constant references to some "Old Pro" were too much for her to take.

"I'm just hopeless," Paul said to himself. Then, with a smile, he said, "I didn't walk the talk—I stumbled the mumble! I could sure use some mulligans right now."

The month flew by and before Paul knew it he was on the plane again heading to Asheville. *I don't see how I can face the Old Pro*, he thought. *After all, I haven't put much of what I learned into practice.*

•   •   •

Solid Shots

I held my tongue when Jake called today with his "life crisis." Quite honestly I think he brings a lot of this crap on himself! I felt like I was a last resort but was able to remain calm while we talked on the phone.

I really don't mind helping him; it's just a bad time. I was about to put into practice some of what the Old Pro has been teaching me, like starting slowly and warming up. Then it hit me, every time Jake has needed me I have missed the opportunity because I was busy. This time I made the time!

My attitude was not perfect, but I think I'm doing the right thing.

I got Jake a flight home and paid for it without blinking. I like that I did that.

I still made my tee time but did not get to stretch or warm up much. When I played poorly (no big surprise), I was able to laugh it off and not get too frustrated. So I guess I'm making a little progress.

Mulligans

I refused a mulligan on the first tee today even though I was rushed and would have loved to say yes, when it was offered. Maybe next time. I can be stubbornly proud.

I'm not very good at warming up before a round of golf or starting my days slowly. This just seems to go against the grain of my life. I'm a high-speed guy. I need to learn how to slow down.

Relationships are hard. Carla's always frustrated with me. People at work can feel the tension when I walk into the room—I can see it on their faces. I'm going to need patience with Jake when he moves in. I feel like I need a whole bucket of mulligans when it comes to my relational world.

CHAPTER 12

MULLIGANS HELP

As Paul drove up to the Muni, the Old Pro was sitting in his familiar place in the rocker on the clubhouse porch. When Paul saw him, his heart filled with joy. All the fear and embarrassment about making so little progress over the past month disappeared at the sight of Will sitting there. He had only been with him three times, but Paul felt he was a caring friend.

Paul knew all too well that he didn't have another real friend—someone he could count on, even trust. As he thought about it, Paul realized he had been friendless for his whole life. His father had abandoned him and his coach had disappointed him. He had been deserted by the two most powerful and important men in his life. They had both taken off, leaving him to fend for himself. Their behavior had damaged his ability to trust anyone who might personally draw close to him. Ever since, he just never had someone in his life he could call a real friend.

Paul certainly didn't look at God in a favorable light. He couldn't imagine God being his friend in the way the Old Pro obviously did.

Paul's mind was going a mile a minute as he parked his car. Before locking it, he grabbed his golf clubs, just in case. As he walked to the clubhouse, the Old Pro's warm smile welcomed him.

"How are you doing, son?"

Paul took a seat next to the Old Pro. "Not as well as I would like to report," he said. "This time it was not only work. My son showed up on my doorstep."

"Really? That's good," said the Old Pro, interested.

"Not exactly," said Paul. "He called first from New York. He had just lost his job and I think he needed a friend. I couldn't believe he thought of me."

"That's great news," said the Old Pro, clapping. "Down deep we all need and want a friend."

"You've been reading my mind!" Paul blurted. Embarrassed by his outburst, he casually added: "Kids are hard to figure out. But losing a job can be a major blow."

Not wanting to let Paul off the hook, the Old Pro said, "Friendship is what love looks like when put into practice. It's having someone who genuinely cares about you and hangs in there with you no matter what."

"I could have used a friend last week with all the turmoil my son caused in my life."

"Turmoil?"

"I lost it when Jake moved in," said Paul. "The hassle of it all sometimes feels like too much for me. To be honest, I wasn't ready to lose some of my freedom. Since Jake arrived, I've struggled to be a real father and friend to him. My girl-friend, Carla, was already complaining about how little time I spent with her. All my focus on Jake was the final straw— she bailed on me. I wasn't happy about that, and I'm afraid I've made Jake feel more like a burden to me than a son."

The Old Pro said to Paul, "Have you ever thought about your father—what he was like and what could have driven him to alcohol?"

"Think about my father!" Paul recoiled. "I might have loved him when he was sober, but I hate him for what he did to my mom and me when he was drinking. No matter how many times he promised to go on the wagon, he always cracked when something tough came his way. I blame him for dying, for leaving us alone and out on a limb. I don't waste my time thinking about him!"

The Old Pro didn't say anything, he just reached over and squeezed Paul's hand.

Something inside of Paul burst open. He couldn't control himself. He began to weep.

"What if your father were here right now?" asked the Old Pro, gently. "What would you want him to say to you?"

Fighting to regain his composure, Paul thought for a moment and said, "Just 'I love you' or 'I am proud of you.'

When he was drinking, he made me feel that if I was out of the way everyone would be happy." Paul ground his teeth. "I swore I would never forgive him. I swore I'd never ever be like him!"

"And …"

"And I'm acting just like my father with my own son." Paul's face filled with pain. "I hate myself for it."

The Old Pro looked directly at Paul and said, "You don't have to let your past with your father or what has happened recently with your son determine the future. You see, the past can help explain the present, but it should never be an excuse for the future. You can forgive your father and yourself and have a second chance with your son.

"Forgiveness is love in action. God has given you a mulligan. He will walk with you and strengthen you as you and your son learn to accept and encourage each other. Your son needs you, Paul. You can turn the tide."

Paul shrugged his shoulders and then looked off into the distance.

After a pause, the Old Pro said, "Sometimes it doesn't just rain, it pours. Yet I know deep down your son really appreciates your giving him a second chance."

Eager to change the subject, Paul lightened his tone and said, "So, given the pressure at work and dealing with my son, the road to hell was paved by good intentions." He chuckled. "I needed some mulligans in my life this last month."

"Speaking of mulligans," said the Old Pro, "why don't you stretch a bit, then loosen up on the putting green and the range, and I'll meet you at the first tee in fifteen minutes. Don't worry about setting your own par. We're going to play a different kind of game today, and this time you'll play all eighteen holes."

Paul took a little longer to warm up than planned. The Old Pro had really gotten to him. He didn't want to face another question that might open the floodgates locked up inside of him.

When Paul finally got to the first tee, the Old Pro was waiting in the driver's seat of the golf cart. "I took a little longer to enter my round," said Paul with a sheepish smile.

"No need to apologize for that," said the Old Pro in a kind voice. "All right Paul, you're going to play eighteen holes. I'm going to watch and drive the cart. There is one new rule for this round: anytime you want to take a mulligan, take it."

"Let me hear that again," said Paul.

"You can take a mulligan on any shot you want."

"I know we've been talking about mulligans in life, but aren't mulligans in golf only allowed for the first tee?"

"Not the way we are going to play today. Not only can you take a mulligan on the first tee, you can take a mulligan on the fairway or out of the trap. If you want to take a putt or a chip over, you can do it. You can take a mulligan anytime, anywhere. Now let's see how well you do."

Paul smiled and said, "This is not my style. I don't take mulligans. But if you insist, I think I'm going to like this game."

On the first tee he smacked a good drive but it ended up in the rough. He shouted, "Mulligan!" and teed up another ball, driving it right down the middle of the fairway.

The Old Pro smiled and said, "Which one are you going to play?"

"That's easy," said Paul with a laugh, "the one in the fairway. You made the rules. I'm going to take advantage of this."

Paul's next shot landed in a sand trap. The Old Pro said, "Give her the old mulligan." This time Paul hit a beautiful shot right into the center of the green. "I'm pretty good, aren't I?" Paul said. "Mulligans really do help."

As they got further into the round, Paul was amazed that he started to take fewer and fewer mulligans. He was swinging with a fluidity and confidence he had never before experienced.

"How do you like playing this way?" asked the Old Pro as they drove away after another of Paul's beautiful shots.

"I love this!" said Paul. "I'm so relaxed—I'm enjoying it."

"That roving mulligan sure helps, doesn't it?"

"Sure does."

As they were driving up the eighteenth fairway, Paul turned to the Old Pro and said, "I'll have to admit this is the most fun I've ever had playing golf."

The Old Pro laughed. "Your score isn't bad, either. If you par this one, you've got a seventy-four. Have you ever shot a seventy-four?"

"I've never broken eighty," Paul admitted.

"Son, you've got that seventy-four in there. You just need to bring it out on the first shot. You are good!"

Paul said, "I'm not good. The mulligan's good."

As they sat together in the golf cart after the round, the Old Pro helped Paul process what had just happened.

"It's amazing," Paul said. "I not only enjoyed the game and scored better, but my confidence kept increasing. I found I wasn't thinking about mechanics. I was just letting the swing flow. I was thinking more about playing golf than playing 'golf swing.' And I certainly wasn't concerned about outcome, because I could always take the shot over if necessary. I hit more good, quality shots in this round than I have hit in any round of my life."

"You sure did," said the Old Pro with a smile. "Having a mulligan to back you up, you proved you could hit all the shots. What if you could take a mulligan any time you wanted in your life?"

"How could I do that?"

"What do you do now if you make a mistake? Say you're impatient. You yell at or ignore an employee, or you make a bad business decision. What happens?"

"I feel awful and I beat myself up," Paul admitted. "Just like I did flying over here. I was down on myself because I didn't follow through with what you have taught me."

"Would you like to know how you could avoid feeling bad when you make a mistake?"

"I sure would."

"Then let's get some lunch and talk about it," urged the Old Pro.

"Great," said Paul. "Let me change my shoes in the locker room and take a little time to write a couple thoughts in my journal. I'll see you in the restaurant in ten minutes."

•   •   •

Solid Shots

Knowing I could receive a mulligan allowed me to perform more easily and with more confidence. I made more solid shots today than any round of my life. I actually want to write down my score. A seventy-four. I know it was with a bunch of mulligans, but I actually believe I could go out and break eighty.

The biggest thing I learned from having an endless source of mulligans is to not beat myself up for my mistakes, but to learn from them. As time went on, I learned from my mistakes naturally, and so I made fewer of them. My confidence grew, my performance got better, and I began to enjoy the game. The big question for me now is how to bring this mulligan philosophy into my life.

Mulligans

If I could live my daily life with endless mulligans, I have a feeling I would have more freedom, make better decisions, and shoot better scores in the game of life. I need to figure this thing out. It makes sense on the golf course, but how does this work in life?

Something inside of me broke open when the Old Pro asked about my dad and my son. I feel embarrassed that I cried in front of Will. I can't remember the last time I shed a tear. But, in some strange way, I think it was a good thing.

I wish I could have a mulligan with Jake. I wish things could really get better between us. I do love that kid. But he frustrates me, too.

That's it for now. I had better go find Will and grab some lunch. He must be wondering what happened to me.

CHAPTER 13

THE ULTIMATE MULLIGAN

PAUL SAT DOWN next to the Old Pro in the lunchroom and they chatted casually for a few minutes.

Finally the Old Pro said, "Maybe we ought to get down to business."

"I like your style," said Paul. "You know, I was thinking in the locker room about how easy it was for me to enjoy playing golf. I played better when I realized that I could always take a mulligan. I'd love to find that ease in my life. Ever since you told me on the first day we met that life is all about relationships, I have become more aware and concerned about my relationships at work, at home, on the golf course—everywhere. I know I could use some mulligans in my life, particularly now that my son is back in the picture—and I'm still letting him down."

The Old Pro smiled. "I was pretty sure you would get to that place. If you want unlimited mulligans in your daily life, it all starts with the Ultimate Mulligan."

"What's the Ultimate Mulligan?" asked Paul.

"It's not a *what*, it's a *who*," said the Old Pro. "It's entering into a relationship with the one who is the originator of the concept of second chances: God."

"Oh, no," said Paul. "As I told you before, I'm not big on religion."

"And neither am I," said the Old Pro, "but I'm big on God. He is the one who invented mulligans. He is all about second chances."

"What's the difference between being religious and what you are talking about?"

"Before I get into that, tell me where you are on your spiritual journey right now—and where you have been."

Paul shrugged. "Pretty simple really—I'm nowhere."

"What do you mean by that?"

"Well, when I was a kid my mom used to drag me off to Sunday school, but I never got too excited about it. We went to a Presbyterian church, and when I got into junior high I switched to the Methodist church, because they had a better basketball team and better-looking girls. That's what I really cared about then—sports and good-looking girls." Paul smiled and continued, "It was at that church I met the basketball coach who let me and everyone else down when he had an affair with a teacher and left town."

"That must have hurt," said the Old Pro. "You have mentioned that coach several times."

"It did," Paul admitted. "And it damaged my faith in God and in other people."

"Why?"

"My coach friend talked to me about his faith all the time and how important it was to be loyal to God first, then your family, and then your friends. And then he goes and has an affair—breaks his wife's heart and devastates his family and friends. That's when I decided I should go it alone."

"Did anybody talk about having a relationship with Jesus?"

"The coach did once in a while, but then he didn't behave much like Jesus. That really bothered me. I saw all kinds of people who went to church on Sunday but during the week they seemed to forget about what they'd learned."

"So you were disappointed in how followers of Jesus behaved," said the Old Pro.

"You got that right," said Paul, "so I stopped even going to church. When I went off to college, people could have cared less about my spiritual growth. I stopped using words like God and Jesus—except on the golf course," Paul said sheepishly.

"Did you ever revisit your faith?" asked the Old Pro.

"When I met my wife, Rebecca," said Paul. "She had been a churchgoer in her youth, so she thought we should get involved in a church, particularly when we had Jake just a year and a half after we got married. As you do early in your marriage, you try to please your wife, so I joined a local church with her. Jake was baptized there, and we would go to church once in a while, especially on Christmas and Easter."

"Did anybody talk about growing a relationship with Jesus at the church?" asked the Old Pro.

"Not really. The pastor preached about God but I never really got into Jesus."

"You got that a little backwards," said the Old Pro with a smile. "Jesus gets into you. But I'll explain that later. Did your wife help you on your journey?"

"She did at first, but then she became disillusioned like me."

"What happened?" asked the Old Pro.

"The pastor of our church was fired after a real political battle. We found out firsthand that some religious people can be vicious, particularly with each other. I liked the pastor. He was my kind of guy. His faith was important to him but he didn't push it on you. He seemed authentic.

"When we saw the politics in the church and the way they treated the pastor," continued Paul, "Rebecca and I said, 'If that's what religion is all about, you can have it.'

"We completely turned our backs on the church. Our pastor friend who got fired tried to convince us not to leave the church even though he, too, had been disappointed with the way people had behaved. I remember he said, 'Churches are full of fallible people. That's why we need a personal relationship with God.' Unfortunately, our marriage started to go south; we weren't able to hear his plea. As you said, it doesn't just rain, it pours."

"Your pastor friend was right," said the Old Pro. "That was not the time or reason to turn your back on God. Would you be interested in finding out more about knowing him?"

"Not really," admitted Paul. "I'm more interested in finding out about mulligans in life."

"Well, God and mulligans go together because he offers the greatest mulligan of all time. After all, he forgives us for our sins—our mistakes. His mulligan works just like a mulligan on the first tee. You can't purchase one—except in charity golf events—or take one by yourself. It has to be offered to you by one of your playing partners. And from the beginning of time, God has wanted to be our life-playing partner."

"I hear what you're saying," said Paul, "but that term 'sin' hits one of my buttons. When I talk to my religious friends, one of the things that has always bugged me is the whole concept of original sin. Why do we have to start off *bad*? Why can't we start off with original potentiality? Then we could be good or bad depending on what we do."

"Let me ask you a question," said the Old Pro. "Do you think you are as good as God?"

"Of course not," snapped Paul. "If there is a God, that's perfection."

"Okay. Let's give God a score of one hundred. Then we'll give axe murderers five. Mother Teresa gets a ninety-five. Now Paul, you are struggling, but you have a good heart and are trying to get out of your own way. I'd give you a sixty-five right now. The striking thing about genuine faith," the Old Pro continued, "is that the Lord sent his Son down to earth to make up the difference between our score and a hundred. That's what grace and forgiveness are all about. It's the Ultimate Mulligan. Because Jesus never sinned and was perfect, he can make up wherever we come short. He can get us to a hundred."

"Why do we have to get a hundred?"

"Let me see if I can explain it this way," said the Old Pro. "God created us to play his course. I like to call it 'The Course Less Played.'"

"Why?"

"Even though it is beautiful, just like the Garden of Eden must have been, it can be difficult. God wants us to play his course by his rules in relationship with him. As a result, most people don't want to play his course, thus the name."

"So we have a choice?"

"Absolutely!" said the Old Pro. "God didn't want us to be robots, so he gave us free will. Just like Adam and Eve, in life we can choose to play our course or his course.

When Adam and Eve chose to play the game their way on their own course, humankind was separated from God. As reported in the Old Testament, they wandered for years, playing their own course with limited success. Though God wasn't pleased about that, he still loved human beings and wanted us all to spend eternity in heaven. But since he is also a just God, he would only permit it if we mended our ways and became perfect—scored one hundred. That, of course, is impossible because the course is difficult and none of us can play that well, not even Ben Hogan."

"Ben Hogan?"

"Yes," said the Old Pro. "Ben was a dear friend of mine. I was greatly saddened when he died some years ago. He was a values-driven man with intense perseverance and a great work ethic. Nobody wanted to perfect the golf swing more than Ben. Even when he was in his eighties he still practiced every day. Shortly after his death, I read an interview in the newspaper by his lovely wife, Valerie. She said what motivated Ben the most was the thought of playing a perfect round. He didn't feel it was out of reach to have eighteen birdies in a row."

"Eighteen birdies in a row—that's unbelievable!" Paul shouted.

"Not any more unbelievable than saying you are a hundred on a one-to-a-hundred scale."

"You got me on that," said Paul. "By the way, I like that one-to-a-hundred concept. It is much better than calling someone a sinner. Besides, I hate labels. When you call somebody a sinner, they get defensive and uptight. But if you ask anyone where they fall on a one-to-a-hundred scale, from imperfection to perfection, nobody would say a hundred. I'm not sure that my score would be much different than the one you gave me. I'd say that I am between sixty and seventy. I'm certainly not perfect. I have a long way to go. Just ask my ex-wife, my son, or the people at work."

"Don't get down on yourself," said the Old Pro. "As I said, we all fall short of perfection, even Ben Hogan."

"I can believe that," said Paul with a laugh, "if eighteen birdies in a row was his goal."

"Well, it was," said the Old Pro. "Valerie went on to say in the interview that Ben had a recurring dream. It really was a nightmare in which he had birdied seventeen holes in a row and was standing on the eighteenth green with a four-foot putt to accomplish this perfect round, but he always missed the putt."

"That certainly would be a nightmare," said Paul.

"Unless you accept help," insisted the Old Pro.

"What kind of help?" asked Paul.

"A relationship with my friend Jesus."

"Here we go again," said Paul with a smile. "Your friend?"

"Yes," said the Old Pro. "Remember earlier I said you had it backwards when you said you didn't get into Jesus?

He wants to be everyone's *friend*. He wants to get to know you."

"Really! Even me?"

"Absolutely," said the Old Pro. "A lot of people don't like the fact that the axe murderer and you get the same shot at the ball as Mother Teresa did. Yet, that's what grace is all about. It's not about deeds; it's about faith. God doesn't grade on a curve. It's a gift. If you accept Jesus as your Savior, no matter what your past has been, he rids you of your sins by making up the difference between your score and one hundred. Jesus got a birdie on every hole. He lived a perfect life and died on the cross in our place. This pivotal event opens the door for us to receive his total forgiveness. None of us can make it to perfection without help. Not even Ben Hogan."

"I didn't know Ben Hogan was such a spiritual leader," said Paul with a chuckle.

"He wasn't," said the Old Pro. "You see, God knows that all of us — including you, me, and Ben Hogan — come short of his perfection. God requires a perfect score- card for us to join him in eternity. So when you turn in your scorecard, if you missed even one putt in an otherwise perfect life, as Hogan always did in his nightmare, then you will miss the cut."

"That's not fair!" stamped Paul.

"No one said it was going to be fair," said the Old Pro with a sincere look on his face. "Remember, it's God's rule, not mine. The Bible says everyone will have to turn in a scorecard at the end of life. We'll be held accountable for the life we have led. People don't like to hear this, but there are no loopholes in the Good Book about this truth. Not only must the scorecard have eighteen birdies on it for one round, but we must birdie every hole we have ever played."

"That's impossible," Paul protested.

"You're right, Paul," soothed the Old Pro. "But what if someone lived a perfect life — birdied every hole he played — and that person offers you his own signed scorecard? All you have to do is attest and sign the card and it becomes yours; you can turn it in on Judgment Day and be home free. You get to go to heaven, which, in golf terms, is like being admitted to the Royal and Ancient."

"The most prestigious golf club in the world? That would be quite a deal," said Paul, "an amazing gift."

"You got that right," said the Old Pro enthusiastically. "And that is exactly what Jesus did when he died on the cross. He paid the price for us. He made up the difference. He played the perfect round and freely offers us his score card."

Paul turned this idea over slowly in his mind.

"Do you know the difference between justice, mercy, and grace?" asked the Old Pro.

"Not really."

"With justice," said the Old Pro, "if you commit a crime, you get the appropriate penalty. With mercy, if you commit a crime, you get less of a penalty than you deserve. With grace, if you commit a crime, someone else takes the penalty. The good news is that God has offered us an incredible gift of eternal life and a restored relationship with him by sending his Son Jesus to pay the penalty for us falling short of a hundred—not making a birdie on every hole we ever played. Because of his Son's death on the cross and his resurrection, God offers us the Ultimate Mulligan in life. As the gospel tells us: Grace is not about you but about the mulligan God has offered through his Son Jesus Christ."

"If I wanted to sign up to take advantage of this Ultimate Mulligan from God, how would I do it?"

"It's really pretty easy. It is the most important action you will ever take," said the Old Pro. "All you've got to do is pray something like:

> Dear God, I know I can't make it to a hundred on my own. Thank you for sending your Son Jesus to live a perfect life and give me the mulligans I need to make it to a hundred. From now on I am ready to move in a new direction with him at my side. I'm ready to play your course and not mine.

"Is that what they have you say in church or at a Billy Graham crusade?" Paul teased the Old Pro.

"Not exactly," came the response, "but the gist is the same. God will know your heart and it's not saying the words in a certain way that counts, it's your sincere attitude. And when that happens you can go to the first tee where you will find a perfect scorecard that is already signed by Jesus. All you have to do is receive your card, attest it, and eternal life is guaranteed. Then Jesus will pick up your bag and you are freely able to play the course with him at your side for the rest of your life. From that time onward you must choose which course you're going to play each day—the old one on your own or the new one with him."

"Will, you really know how to paint a clear picture. Thanks," said Paul. "Still, my problem is, if I sign up, I'm afraid I won't follow through on my commitment."

The Old Pro took a scorecard out of his back pocket and pulled out a pencil. He wrote on the scorecard the words "commitment" and "follow through." Then he crossed them out. "God already knows you can't keep your commitment," he said. "He knows that you can't follow through. That is why you need his gift of a mulligan. Remember how you had to use a lot of mulligans in the beginning of your round when you could take a mulligan any time you wanted? You were still making mistakes. That's the way your life will be after you pray and tee it up on the first tee of his course."

"In other words, I will still goof?" wondered Paul.

"Absolutely," said the Old Pro. "But remember, as you played further into your round you didn't need as many mulligans."

"Right," said Paul. "I was relaxed and into the flow of the game."

"It will be the same with your life as you develop a stronger relationship with Jesus. He offers you unlimited mulligans in your life. His presence will make you relax and help you stay on track without needing his forgiveness—a mulligan—as often." The Old Pro turned over the scorecard and wrote on the back:

Accept and receive, because
grace is a gift that you are given.

"Now I get the picture," said Paul. "I need a caddy for my game of life just like I need a caddy for golf. Still, I bet we have to make our own tee-off time, show up and be ready to play, and stick the tee in the ground."

"You've got that right," said the Old Pro. "When you show up to play God's course, Jesus through the Holy Spirit is waiting on the first tee, ready to grab your bag and guide you around the course that his Father laid out—The Course Less Played. You have to stick the tee in the ground and hit the first shot. But don't worry, Jesus will walk with you and be there for every shot you play. His course is now yours to play, but *you have to play the shots.* He won't play them for you, even though he is available for support and counsel. Therefore, before each shot or decision you make, talk it over and strategize with him."

"Wow!" said Paul, honestly impressed. "That would be like having a friend like you always by my side as my caddy."

"Absolutely," said the Old Pro. "As a matter of fact, he is a better friend than I could ever be—and a smarter caddy."

"I find that hard to believe," said Paul.

"Well, it's true; you will learn this with time," assured the Old Pro.

"You certainly don't see many caddies around golf courses today, do you?" Paul observed.

"That's true," said the Old Pro. "Originally golf was meant to be played as a two-man team: the player and his caddy. The caddy knew the course and he knew the player's strengths and weaknesses. He knew how far the player could hit various clubs. There were many blind shots on the links of the past. Thus, it was the responsibility of the caddy to show the player where to aim and fire. The player had to trust the caddy with his total game. They worked as a team."

"I brushed off my caddie on the first hole during the Pro-Am with Davis Love," said Paul with a smile.

"I would have guessed as much," said the Old Pro. "And yet the sorrowful thing about that was he just happens to be the number-one caddie at the course. He could have guided you around beautifully."

"So you are suggesting that golf is not made to be played alone. And life is not meant to be lived alone," said Paul thoughtfully.

"Absolutely," insisted the Old Pro. "The caddy worked with the player like a coach. Without that, it's no wonder the handicap for the average golfer in America has gone up rather than down over the last twenty years! Those electric golf carts have ruined the way the game was meant to be played. It saddens me to see how golfers today play all by themselves. After you get dropped off by your cart-mate, you stand alone and must prepare and hit your shot without any help. You can see how far we have come away from the original, wonderful design of the game."

"As well as the original design of the game of life," smiled Paul.

"I think you're catching on," said the Old Pro, grinning. "Are you ready to sign up and accept and receive your teammate?"

"I hear what you're saying," said Paul. "You've made more sense than anything I've heard before about having a relationship with God. But I'm not sure I'm ready to sign up."

"I figured you weren't," said the Old Pro. "Some people say that following Jesus and the instructions he gives to his pupils are for the weak. But that is not the truth. The toughest test of self-esteem is bowing your head and saying, 'Dear Lord, I cannot make it to a hundred without you. I can't score the perfect round.' Our ego doesn't want to admit that or give up control."

"I'm listening," said Paul.

"The first sin was *not* murder, adultery, or any other action we commonly label as sin. The first sin was—and still is—the desire to be one's own god, to control one's own life, and to be in charge."

"I've sure seen that," said Paul.

"Don't you worry," said the Old Pro, "we'll have future lessons. The big one I want to leave you with today is that you have a chance to have the Ultimate Mulligan in your life—someone who will forgive you for your bad shots, someone who will forgive you for your mistakes, someone who will forgive you for your transgressions, and someone who will stand beside you and never leave you."

Paul looked downward with a thoughtful gaze.

"Remember forgiveness is love in action," continued the Old Pro. "God unconditionally loves you and knows you can't be perfect without a relationship with Jesus. All Jesus wants you to do is to reach out to him in good times and in bad times. As he promises at the end of the book of Matthew, he will be with us until the end of the age. In other words, he is only a whisper away for help. See you next time. In the meantime, if you are ready to tee it up on God's course, give me a call."

"You'll be the first to know," said Paul with a smile.

•   •   •

Solid Shots

While we talked at lunch and afterward, the Old Pro explained the whole "Ultimate Mulligan" thing. I really listened. I think I have the basic concept. I feel good about my ability to grasp what he was talking about. It all sounds a bit religious to me, but I appreciate that Will is sincere about his faith.

In some ways, the idea of the Ultimate Mulligan and having a life-caddy who is better than the Old Pro seems too good to be true. What if I could have a perfect score?

Here is what I gleaned from Will's insights on playing the perfect round and getting the Ultimate Mulligan:

- We all fall short of a hundred; only God is perfect.
- God requires a perfect round and we all fall short of that score.
- He sent his Son Jesus to play the perfect round for us — eighteen birdies.
- Jesus died on the cross for everyone, paid the penalty, and was resurrected. In essence, Jesus signed the card. All we have to do is attest to it and we get to turn it in as our own perfect round. That gives us a place in heaven and a lifetime caddy. That's what grace and forgiveness are all about.
- God's Ultimate Mulligan is ours through a friendship with Jesus. He gives us second chances every day, from the first tee to the last hole.
- God's course is not designed for the weak. One of the toughest tests of self-esteem is to bow your head and admit to the Lord you can't handle everything by yourself.

- Jesus wants to be my caddy and he could help me play the game of life. Just as in golf, life was not meant to be played alone.

Mulligans

I have played alone for too long. On the golf course and in life, I have not let anyone be a caddy for me. Except for Old Will Dunn, I don't even have friends. I want to start over in my relational life. I need some mulligans here.

I like the idea of the Ultimate Mulligan and having a caddy at my side, one I can actually trust. I am going to chew on this in the coming week. A lot of what Will says makes sense. Some of it seems a bit out there. I believe the Old Pro means well. I like him a lot and I trust him. I just don't know if I can trust what he is saying. If he is right, then WOW! If he is wrong, then I guess he's just crazy or misinformed.

CHAPTER 14

THE FIRST
TEE SHOT

OVER THE NEXT FEW WEEKS Paul thought hard about all the Old Pro had taught him about mulligans and a relationship with Jesus. He reread his journal notes and was struck by how much he was learning about life and golf.

For the first time, faith in God was beginning to make sense to Paul. Still, he was not ready to bow his head, step onto the tee, and take the Ultimate Mulligan, even after two more visits with the Old Pro.

What Paul loved about Will was that he didn't push him. He really was a friend who was willing to walk beside Paul, listen to him, and not judge. By his actions the Old Pro taught him the truth that friendship is what love looks like when it is put into practice.

The more time Paul spent with the Old Pro, the more he realized that Jesus wanted to be that kind of friend to us all. *Why am I so reluctant to admit I could use help from a friend like Jesus?* thought Paul. *I don't have to carry my own bag or drag a cart anymore.*

"Don't be hard on yourself," said the Old Pro on one of their visits. "Be patient. It will happen when it is meant to happen."

The Old Pro was right again. It did happen, but not for about a year. Paul was dealing with a top-management selection problem. He had always felt that he was more of a visionary leader — providing direction — than someone who wanted to or could run day-to-day operations. As a result, he searched for a president and COO to lead his company on a daily basis.

The executive he had appointed, while having great knowledge of business and many of the necessary skills, had a very different set of operational values, especially since Paul had been meeting and learning from his friend the Old Pro.

In the past, Paul had been a seagull manager. If he delegated to one of his people, he would leave him or her alone until he or she made a mistake. Then he would fly in like a seagull, make a lot of noise, dump on this person, and fly out.

During one of their visits the Old Pro had convinced Paul that this was not a good way to manage others or his golf game. "So many people don't pat themselves on the back or praise themselves on the golf course. They just react when they make a mistake," said the Old Pro. "We treat people at work the same way. The only way they know whether they are doing a good job or not is if no one has yelled at them lately. They soon learn that no news is good news."

"How do you overcome that tendency?"

"You have to establish a set of operating values and goals," said the Old Pro. "Then wander around and see if you can catch anyone doing something right. Accentuate the positive."

Finally, Paul realized the nature of his past shortcomings. It amazed even the Old Pro when Paul, Mr. Type A, who always strove to be the best and achieve the most, decided to establish a set of operating values for his company with *integrity* as the number one value, followed by *relationships*, *success*, and *learning*. The Old Pro convinced Paul to rank those values because, as he said, "Life is about value choices. Sometimes you can't do two values at the same time."

The executive Paul had appointed as president and COO bought into the success value and wanted to make the company mean, lean, and profitable. The integrity and relationships values carried little weight with him. Since he wasn't open to feedback, learning was not a high priority either. As a result, he was wreaking havoc with Paul's people. The new Paul did not appreciate that.

Paul teed up with the Lord one night as he was driving to meet Jake to seek his advice, counsel, and support on this matter (yes, Jake!). Paul and his son had some rocky times when Jake first moved to Atlanta, but after Paul had talked with the Old Pro about having a second chance — a mulligan — with his son, he had truly reached out to him. Paul was even able to talk with Jake about his alcoholic father — the grandfather Jake had never known.

Sharing his vulnerabilities with his son began the healing process between them. Paul had grown to appreciate his son's thinking. Jake had gotten a good job with another manufacturing company in quality control. Paul thought he was a darned-good businessman for a young man. He was proud of him. He found himself more and more naturally giving Jake the counsel, love, and praise his son so longed to have. In fact, he was planning to have dinner with Jake that night.

On the way to meet Jake, Paul realized he was getting a headache from thinking so hard about the problem with the COO. Suddenly he got a blinding flash of the obvious: *Why was he trying to figure this out all by himself?* As the Old Pro had said, "Help is a prayer away."

That moment Paul said to the Lord, "I can't bow my head completely now because I'm driving, but I can't figure out all this stuff by myself. My score falls short of a hundred; I am ready to play the course you have laid out for me. But I need help. I accept your Son Jesus as my savior, Lord, teacher, friend, caddy for life, and my bridge between you and me."

The minute he made that decision and spoke those words, Paul could feel positive energy moving through his body. When he got to the restaurant and walked in, his son looked up from the table.

"What happened to you?" he asked. "You look different."

When Paul told his son about his decision that night, Jake was happy for his father but still skeptical about pursuing his own relationship with Jesus. Raising his eyebrows, Jake asked, "Dad, how will this make a difference in your life?"

Paul swallowed hard and then reached across the table and took Jake's hand. "I want to start by asking your forgiveness. I hated my father because he abandoned me and then I did the same thing to you. That is a burden on my heart that I've been living with ever since the Old Pro got my attention and made me look at my life. Can I ever make it up to you? I love you, Jake, and wish I had been a better father to you all these years."

With that, Jake began to cry. The unimaginable was happening. Type-A Paul was holding his son's hand and they were crying together.

When they both regained their composure, Jake said, "Dad, what you just did and said goes way beyond any sermon I have ever heard."

"Jake, being here with you now is exactly where I need to be," Paul said. "I know I have a long way to go, and I can't think of a better way to start this new journey than to be with you. Thanks for giving your old man a second chance — we have a lot of catching up to do." Then, getting back into his head, he said, "I recently read that the next great evangelistic movement will be demonstration. If you want somebody to be interested in the Lord, you ought to behave differently."

"I believe that," said Jake. "Talking about demonstration, what are you going to do about your top manager?"

"I'm going to talk to him tomorrow in a caring but firm way," insisted Paul. "I am convinced that with Jesus as my caddy, what needs to happen will happen."

That night when Paul got home, he left a message on the Old Pro's answering machine. "I did it!" he said. "I signed up for Jesus as my lifetime caddy. Let's talk. I still need more strategies for bringing the Ultimate Mulligan into my life on a day-to-day basis." Before going to bed, Paul picked up his journal and recorded his life-changing decision.

When he sat down with his COO the next day, they talked frankly together. Paul told him what he liked about his leadership style and praised him. Then he told him what he wanted to happen differently and redirected him. In the end, the COO said, "Paul, I appreciate your honesty but I am not sure I can live up to your expectations. I am a bottom-line guy just like you used to be. I don't care whether people love me or I them. That doesn't matter to me. I expect people to perform; I'm not here to hold their hands. Why don't we call it a photo finish between your firing me and my quitting?" The two men laughed, and then Paul said, "That sounds fair to me, but I want you to know that I will see you are taken care of until you get another opportunity."

•   •   •

Solid Shots

I made the best shot of my life today!

I did it. I asked Jesus to forgive all my mistakes. I still don't like the word "sin," but I guess I can say that Jesus took away my sins. He is my caddy and my friend. I feel like a new man.

The Old Pro was right. It happened at the right time. No one had to force me.

To top it off, I started a transition plan with my COO and I did it the right way. I did the right thing the right way. That was a solid shot.

I feel a new connection with Jake. We are starting a whole new chapter. Things are going to change between us. I know they are.

I feel like Jesus is right next to me pointing out the hazards, giving me the right club, helping me each moment. Who would have dreamed I would be where I am today?

Not me! But I love it. I can't wait to talk with the Old Pro and tell him the good news.

Mulligans

I see things very differently now. I am excited for the future. Having this friendship with Jesus has opened my eyes to the fact that I have been a real jerk in the ways I have treated people. I am so glad God offers me unlimited mulligans, because I need them.

CHAPTER 15

THE COURSE
LESS PLAYED

PAUL COULD NOT WAIT to visit the Old Pro to personally share the new decision he had finally made to step up to the first tee. It was a whole new way of looking at life, and he was excited to hear what the Old Pro would say about how to move forward and play the new course laid out before him.

On the outbound flight, Paul reflected again on the incredible blessing that the Old Pro had been in his own life—how he had given him a whole new way to look at things and an inner strength to live life as he knew he should. He couldn't wait to get off the plane and drive over to the Muni as soon as possible.

As he pulled the car into the parking lot, he could see Will sitting patiently on his rocker. As he approached the

Old Pro his heart began to race. Old Will Dunn had truly become the father he had never known and someone whom he longed to be with. As soon as their eyes met, tears of joy began to well up in both of them. The Old Pro rose to his feet and embraced his young apprentice with a hug, an act Paul would never forget. No words were needed; the hug said it all. Just like his cry with his son the night he turned his life over to the Lord, this hug was an embrace that Paul had longed for all of his life—a warm, loving, and accepting embrace. It meant the world to Paul, and he did not want to let go.

At last they sat down, and the Old Pro turned and said, "Paul, I'm so glad that you made this pivotal decision to tee it up with God and seek to play His course."

"Where do we go from here with my life—and golf?" asked Paul.

"So you're still interested in golf," said the Old Pro with a laugh. "Let me grab Old Faithful." He stood up, grabbed his putter, and said, "Follow me."

Paul followed him down the steps. They walked to the left of the clubhouse past the putting green to the tenth tee. The tenth hole was a long par four that wound through a row of tall oaks and pines on either side. Playing this hole was almost like stepping into a cathedral. The scene was quiet and majestic.

As they stood on the tee the Old Pro picked up Old Faithful, pointed it down the fairway, and said, "Paul, what do you see out there?"

Paul said, "I just see huge trees and all kinds of trouble. If I hit into those trees on the right, there will be no way to get back onto the fairway. But if I hook to the left, I'm in jail. There's no shot to the green."

The Old Pro said, "Now that's no way to look at this hole. There is a whole new way to look at this hole — as well as your life."

"Really?" said Paul.

"Yes," said the Old Pro. "Did you know that the human mind and the computer have something in common? Neither the computer nor the mind knows the difference between what is true and what you tell them. If you put information into a computer, it won't say 'Where did you get your information? Your figures are wrong.' You've probably heard it said about the computer: 'garbage in ...'"

" ... garbage out," Paul chimed.

"Absolutely," said the Old Pro. "The mind is the same way. If, when you woke up this morning, you looked into the mirror and said, 'You're fabulous,' your mind would not say, 'Who are you kidding? I know you much better than that.'"

"I'm sure it wouldn't," said Paul with a chuckle.

"So if the mind does not know the difference between the truth and what you tell it, would it be better to program your mind with positive thoughts or negative thoughts?"

"Positive thoughts, obviously."

"Okay then, would it be better on this hole to think about hitting a beautiful drive right down the middle of the fairway or hooking one into the woods on the left?"

"You're suggesting I shouldn't even think about the woods," said Paul, triumphantly.

"Absolutely," said the Old Pro. "And don't think about results either."

"Results?" questioned Paul. "I shouldn't think about results?"

"Maybe not," said the Old Pro with a suggestive smile. "Some of the best amateur golfers I've worked with develop a NATO attitude toward golf."

"NATO?" said Paul.

"Yes, NATO. It stands for **N**ot **A**ttached **T**o **O**utcome. That doesn't mean that these people are not interested in hitting good shots or scoring well, but they are not their scores. They are not each shot. As a result, they're more relaxed and able to swing freely at the ball without fear. When you're attached to outcome, you become fearful of your results.

"In the process you begin to program your mind with negative thoughts. You start saying things such as, 'Don't hit it in the water,' or, 'Don't hit it out of bounds.' Not knowing the difference between the truth and what you tell it, the mind doesn't understand the word *don't*. So when you say, 'Don't hit it in the trees,' all the mind hears is: 'Hit it in the trees.' Instead, you should concentrate on where you want to go—the middle of the fairway—rather than where you do not want to go—the trees. When you are focused on something positive and have a target or goal in mind without concern for outcome, you will perform better."

"I once heard a speaker at a convention say to everyone, 'Don't think about pink elephants. No matter what you do, don't think about pink elephants,'" Paul said. "Then he asked everyone, 'What are you thinking about right now?'"

"Pink elephants!" said the Old Pro, chuckling. "That's a perfect example of what I'm talking about."

"If I start to think about the trees, what should I do?"

"Back off your shot. Imagine them as friends stretching their arms out and pointing you to the fairway. They give definition to the hole."

"Interesting!"

"Once you see the golf course from this perspective, then you can begin to build positive images in your mind instead of negative responses," said the Old Pro. "As I've suggested, the mind cannot differentiate between a negative and a positive picture. It just sees the picture and tries to direct your body toward the target."

"It's the same way in life, isn't it?" wondered Paul.

"Absolutely," said the Old Pro. "When you get into difficult relationships with people or circumstances, you need to see them as friends, not enemies. They are just God's way of helping you to focus your attention in the right direction. When Jack Nicklaus was on the top of his game, he was one of the greatest generals on the golf course when it came to strategizing and focusing. Before taking a swing, Jack would stand behind his ball and look down the fairway with his mind strategically thinking of the shot. He called this 'going to the movies.'"

"What does that mean?" asked Paul.

"He imagined himself in a movie theater, watching himself play the shot at hand and pull it off exactly the way he had envisioned it," the Old Pro replied. "Then, as he made his practice swing, he imagined himself playing that very shot. He stepped into the shot, lined up with his immediate target, and let it fly just as he had envisioned it in his mind."

"That's interesting," said Paul. "I assume he did that on every shot?"

"He sure did," said the Old Pro. "There is a story about Jack when he was playing a strategic shot in a big tournament. It was a number of years ago, when they used to mike the players to catch any conversation between them and maybe hear some of the positive self-talk that was going on. Jack, after going to the movies, approached the shot from behind. Just as he was beginning to pull back the club, a plane flew over his head. The distraction made him stop and under his breath you could hear him say, 'Now that was a good one.' You see, he had already played his shot in his mind. He was just going through the motions."

"So on this hole, the trees would not even be part of his picture."

"They sure wouldn't be," said the Old Pro. Then with a warm smile he continued, "Paul, this is the way you need to learn to play your shots and also live your life. In golf, first focus your mind on where you want the ball to go — then the shot you want to play. As you select a club, focus on the shot you desire to play and how you are going to execute that shot. Then go to your bag and pick out the club that will get you strategically to the position that you desire. Next, always take a practice swing in the direction you want to go. That helps you put that imprint into your mind and you've got a better chance of pulling off the shot."

"That's great," said Paul. "I'd like to do that every time I play a shot from now on."

"Good idea," the Old Pro said. "Here's a simple way to remember it. For every shot you must go to the movies. Visualize with your mind's eye the shot that you want to play. Take a practice swing and experience the shot. Then commit and trust the shot. It's as easy as 1 – 2 – 3. Visualize, practice, and commit."

"Absolutely," said Paul.

"Now take your practice swing and get focused on the shot you want to play. Take time to let your muscles get in touch with what your mind is seeing in your mental movie. Now take a practice swing and feel the shot."

"Got that now," said Paul.

"Okay, Paul, now set up to the ball, get ready, and free-wheel it down the middle. That's when the trust comes in."

Paul nailed it right down the center.

"That's it, son!" the Old Pro exclaimed, pumping his fist. "You've got it!"

Paul was beaming. "I get how this works for golf, but what about life?" he asked. "How does that concept relate?"

"It all comes down to entering your day slowly," said the Old Pro. "As you look at your day, focus on what you want to accomplish, not on the obstacles that might be in your way. Imagine yourself sitting on your bed at night, smiling because you've had a productive day. Then when the day presents itself and you see some obstacles, such as trees to the right or water to the left, you can focus back on the plan that you've already contemplated. You need to see these obstacles as markers guiding you in the direction you want to go."

"I'm beginning to see it," said Paul.

"Good!" said the Old Pro. "And remember, now you have a good friend and caddy in your life, Jesus, to discuss things with along the way. That is what he wants from you: your attention and your friendship. It is that friendship that will transform your life, Paul. It is up to us to look at life as an adventure—just as we look at each hole in golf as a new adventure—and play it shot by shot, planning and executing each shot to the best of our ability with his help. We simply trust the image we have created together and let it go."

"Thanks," said Paul. "I'm eager to put today's lesson into practice in my life."

Back on the plane to Atlanta, Paul found himself thanking God for the tremendous gift the Lord had given him in the person of the Old Pro. He reflected on how in the few days since he had received the pivotal mulligan he was already experiencing the new life and perspective the Old Pro had talked about. Many of the lessons the Old Pro had taught him were starting to really click. He could see what Will had been talking about.

These truths were becoming a reality, and he recognized that he was being transformed, not only by his friendship with the Old Pro, but more importantly, by an inner desire to share more of his life with this *friend* of the Old Pro. He found himself mentally talking to Jesus as a friend, caddie, and brother. He saw how this simple inner dialogue with Jesus and receiving his unlimited mulligans could transform his life. His old performance-based attitude no longer had to dictate his life.

Paul pulled his journal from his briefcase and mused, I think I'm ready to play this new course laid out before me!

·   ·   ·

Solid Shots

The Old Pro had great advice for making solid shots as I walk The Course Less Played. This stuff is gold! I need to remember these simple ideas and I will hit some great shots in the game of life:

- Garbage in, garbage out. I need to adjust my thinking and keep my mind on positive things and not the negative. My mind is a computer and I need to feed it positive data. This will lead to solid shots in golf and life.
- I want to have a NATO attitude toward golf and life: **N**ot **A**ttached **T**o **O**utcomes.
- Life and faith are as simple as 1−2−3. I need to visualize, practice, and then commit. This simple process will keep my shots flying down the center of the fairway.
- Jesus is my friend and caddy. I can trust him all the time. When I listen to him and follow his counsel, my whole life will change.

Mulligans

I have put a lot of garbage into my mental computer over the years. And this has led to a lot of garbage coming out. With Jesus as my caddy and a mulligan any time I need one, I am going to watch what I put into my mind. I am committed to thinking positive thoughts and refusing to let the negative take over my thinking and attitudes.

CHAPTER 16

THE PHONE CALL

PAUL KEPT IN CONTACT with the Old Pro over the next few years. His friend proved extremely helpful in providing Paul with strategies for bringing the Ultimate Mulligan into his life on a day-to-day basis. The Old Pro became the friend Paul never had, and in many ways, a father too. Every time Paul traveled to Asheville to see the Old Pro, it was a joyful occasion. They talked heart-to-heart about life, his son, his new friend Jesus, and, of course, golf.

As for his golf game, Paul never seemed to break that barrier and reach the illusive single-digit handicap he had always wanted, but he sure had more fun, enjoyed the fellowship, and developed an appreciation for the beauty around him. His golf score never again had the same power over Paul that it had when he first met the Old Pro.

One day in the early spring, Paul felt a special urge to talk with the Old Pro. He phoned him a number of times but got no answer. If that wasn't strange enough, his friend's answering machine wasn't working. Even if he didn't get the Old Pro on the phone, Paul always loved to listen to his message:

Life is a very special occasion. I hope you don't miss it. Sorry I have missed your call. Please leave a friendly message. May God bless you today. And remember: God loves you and so do I.

Every time Paul heard that message, he pictured the Old Pro and it brought a smile to his face.

Paul had never asked the Old Pro where he lived, so he was not sure how to track him down. In an odd sort of way, Old Will Dunn seemed completely at home at the golf course, in his chair near the club house, lingering around the practice area and teaching kids to putt on the practice green or on the course with a friend.

Paul had always called ahead and planned a time to visit. But after a number of attempts to contact the Old Pro, he decided to fly over to Ashville and check in on his dear friend.

• • •

Solid Shots

The past few years have been amazing. Life is not perfect, but it is great. I think more positively. My relationships are stronger. I enjoy almost every round of golf—although I can still let a bad round get under my skin more than it should. Jesus is my caddy and closest friend. And I am learning to play the course Jesus has set before me. I can still hook or slice a shot at any given moment as I walk through this life, but I am hitting more solid shots than ever before.

Mulligans

Two growth areas seem to be an ongoing reminder that I still need mulligans on a regular basis.

First, I can ramp up and rev my motor at the red line if I am not careful. I love starting my day slowly and am getting better at it. But on any given day I can shift into overdrive and rush right past my time with Jesus. Lord, help me slow down and make the discipline of making space for you each morning become a natural part of every day.

Second, the opinions of others can still have more influence on me than they should. I need to be careful that Jesus is my caddy and that the expectations and opinions of others don't drive my decisions and actions.

CHAPTER 17

"WELL DONE, WILL DUNN!"

THE NEXT DAY, Paul cancelled all his meetings and took the familiar short flight to Asheville. As he drove over to the Muni in search of the Old Pro, Paul reflected on the past years and what they had meant to him, to his family, and even to his golf game.

About four blocks from the course Paul realized there must be a tournament going on. There were cars parked on both sides of the road. He sighed, thinking about the fact that he did not really want to take a long walk to the course. But when he pictured the Old Pro starting the day slowly and taking a leisurely stroll, Paul adjusted his attitude.

As he walked into the parking lot of the Muni, he saw that his suspicions were correct. There was a huge crowd gathered around the eighteenth green.

Paul found himself walking a little faster, hoping he could see the final putt fall. He kept waiting to hear a roar, or a collective sigh if the putt was missed, but the crowd remained silent.

It must be the trophy ceremony, Paul thought to himself, a little disappointed. *I missed it!*

Paul worked his way into the back of the crowd and tried to look over the people to see who was receiving the trophy. He gently nudged a gentleman standing next to him and whispered, "Who won?"

"What do you mean?" the man whispered back.

Paul said, "This is a trophy ceremony, right? Who won? Who got the trophy?"

The gentleman looked at Paul for a moment, as if he were gathering his words carefully. "I guess you could say Will Dunn won."

Paul was confused, "I don't get it."

The gentleman said, "This is a memorial service for Ol' Will Dunn. He passed away three days ago. Everyone around here called him the Old Pro. Did you know him?"

The words took the wind right out of Paul. He glanced back at the rocking chair still sitting on the porch of the club where he had visited with the Old Pro so many times over the past few years. He looked over toward the driving range, straining his eyes, hoping he would see his old friend. Then his vision got blurry as hot tears began to form in his eyes.

Paul swallowed hard and said, "Yeah, I knew him. He was my friend, kind of like a dad. He was *my* Old Pro." To his surprise, Paul didn't feel embarrassed about his tears.

It helped that the gentleman next to him was a bit choked up, too. He looked at Paul and said two simple words: "Me, too!"

About that time someone up on the eighteenth green said a prayer and thanked everyone for coming. No one seemed to want to leave. They just hung around the green and began conversations, mostly about the Old Pro.

Paul wandered off by himself, walking down the eighteenth fairway toward the tee. He reflected on all that the Old Pro had meant to him. He smiled as he thought about what had led to their first meeting. He thought, *I have come a long way.* As he turned and walked slowly back toward the green, he was filled with a deep thankfulness for the Old Pro, for Jesus his caddy, and for the reality of daily mulligans.

Most of the people were still lingering around the eighteenth green talking together. Paul noticed the man he had spoken to earlier and went to formally introduce himself. "I'm Paul, nice to meet you. How did you know the Old Pro?"

"Good to meet you, too. Sorry it had to be under these circumstances. I met Will after a Pro-Am at the Biltmore Forest I played in two years ago. I'm a little embarrassed to say it, but I did not handle myself very well and the touring pro in my group introduced me to Will after the round. Since then I have stopped by here every time I travel within a hundred miles. I have learned more from Will about golf, life, and God's love than I could tell you."

Paul didn't know if he should laugh or cry. He asked, "Was the golf pro Davis Love?"

With a surprised look the man asked, "How did you know?"

Paul went on to tell his story about meeting the Old Pro, and they both shared a moment of amazement and joy together. They talked about how they both had learned about the mulligan, starting their days slowly, The Course Less Played, and living each day with Jesus as their caddy.

As they wrapped up their conversation, the gentleman asked Paul, "Did you see the trophy and the scorecard?" Paul reminded him that he came late and didn't know anything about a scorecard or trophy. The gentleman pointed to some tables off to the side of the eighteenth green and said, "Just take a look up there."

Paul hurried over to have a look. On top of the table was a scorecard. Paul looked at it more closely and saw that there was a birdie on every hole. It was the perfect score! The card was signed by Jesus and attested by Will Dunn. Written across the bottom of the card was a note in Will's handwriting:

See you in the clubhouse, my friends, at the Royal and Ancient. Until then, God bless you.

Paul broke into a huge smile as his mind was flooded with memories of his friend. He felt peaceful and confident that he would see him again some day. Then Paul looked at the trophy on the table and read the simple inscription.

"Well done, Will Dunn, good and faithful servant."

Paul smiled. Those were the words the Old Pro had wanted to hear at the end of his life. *I know you've heard those words*, Paul thought, *and I want to hear them some day, too!*

As Paul turned from the trophy table, he realized there were still a number of people talking, telling stories, laughing, and crying together. Noticing a man standing by himself a short distance away, Paul wandered over and said, "Hi, I'm Paul. How did you know the Old Pro?"

"Good to meet you. My story is kind of funny. I'm not even a golfer! I met Will one morning when I was walking my dog. He was taking his morning stroll, using a golf club as a walking stick, and he looked like the most content person in the world. We just ended up walking and talking together and before I knew it he was helping me learn how to start my days slowly. Over the last ten years we became friends and I learned so much from him. I didn't even know what a mulligan was the first time I met the Old Pro, but now I have the Ultimate Mulligan. I use mulligans all the time—and I don't even golf."

Over the next twenty minutes, Paul had a number of similar conversations. His heart was filled with joy as he realized that Ol' Will Dunn had been an Old Pro to so many people. There were young kids who had taken putting lessons from the Old Pro. There was a group of people from the local city mission who knew Will from the times he came and served at the soup kitchen. There were bankers, farmers, housewives, and doctors.

For some reason, it had never struck Paul that the Old Pro had many friends. When they got together, Paul felt like he was the most important person in the world to the Old Pro. And, at that moment, he realized he was.

CHAPTER 18

ON THE PORCH

As Paul began to walk away from the eighteenth green, he saw a young man on the porch in front of the club-house. He was sitting right next to the rocking chair that the Old Pro always sat in when he and Paul talked. He walked slowly toward the young man, thinking, *The Old Pro would stop and talk to this guy. Maybe I should, too.*

"Hi, I'm Paul."

The young man looked up, "Good to meet you. I'm Tim."

This kid looks more like a surfer than a golfer, Paul thought. But he said, "How did you know the Old Pro?"

The young man told his story: "I only met him three weeks ago. I have a dream of becoming a PGA teaching pro and a buddy of mine told me I had to meet Mr. Dunn. When I drove down here we just hit it off. I've never been real close to my dad and the Old Pro was so kind and encouraging. I guess I was excited because I felt like I had a new friend and thought that Mr. Dunn might be able to help me with my life."

The young man continued, "He started telling me about how golf and life have a lot in common. He mentioned that there is an Ultimate Mulligan and a Course Less Played, but we were going to talk more about that today. When I drove down today, I didn't even know he had passed away."

Paul looked down at the young man, who was sitting in the same chair Paul had sat in so many times over the past few years. Then he glanced at the Old Pro's rocking chair sitting open in front of him. He thought, *I wonder if it would be inappropriate for me to sit in Will's chair?* But Paul felt a strong urge to talk with this young man. As Paul sat down in the rocking chair, he looked at Tim and saw longing in his eyes. The young man seemed like he had a few pieces of a puzzle but needed more.

Without really thinking about it, Paul said, "Have you ever heard anyone say, 'Golf means **G**ame **O**f **L**ife **F**irst'?"

Tim shook his head. "No."

Paul began to share some of the lessons he had learned from the Old Pro. He began to tell about the Ultimate Mulligan and The Course Less Played. He admitted that he had made his fair share of mistakes, but with the help of the old Pro he had a whole new outlook on life. Paul was careful not to push Tim or go too fast. Even as he was talking, he kept having flashbacks to how the Old Pro had walked slowly with him, moving with Paul at his own pace.

After talking a while, the young man said, "You know so much about life. You have it all together!"

Paul chuckled and said, "You would not have said that four years ago."

Tim stared off toward the eighteenth green for a moment and then looked right at Paul. "You can say no if you want to, I would understand. But, well, is there any way we could get together and talk some more?"

Paul was stunned by the question. For a moment he did not know what to say. All kinds of thoughts raced through his mind. *This kid is asking me to be his Old Pro. I need an Old Pro in my life. I'm not Old Pro material. I don't even have a single digit handicap.*

What came out of his mouth was, "I would be honored!"

As Paul spoke these words, he thought, *What have I just committed to do?* But, something deep inside told him that, with Jesus as his caddy, he might just have something to offer.

Paul chuckled and asked, "If we are going to get together, I should know where you call home." When Tim answered "Atlanta," a grin broke out on Paul's face. "Believe it or not that's where I live!" They both had a good laugh and Paul invited this young lad to join him at his club for a round of golf and to continue their new friendship.

Later, as Paul walked back to his car, he could sense that there really was a larger purpose for his life. *Maybe some things really are just meant to be*, he thought.

On the way to the airport he passed by the entrance to the Biltmore Forest Club, where he had met the old Pro for the first time. He couldn't help but pull over into the parking lot and stroll up onto the porch where he'd first met his mentor. He basked in the glory of the golf course that lay before him with its towering trees and lush green fairways. Never had he appreciated the beauty and peacefulness of God's creation like this until he met the Old Pro.

As he looked down toward that infamous ninth green he thought, *I can't believe one of the most embarrassing nine holes of golf I ever played turned into one of the most beneficial. The most important advice I ever received from a golf pro was from Davis Love III that day, and he didn't say a word about my swing.* His goal that day had been to leverage a relationship with Davis Love to further his golf game. Instead, Davis — knowing Paul had a bigger problem than just his golf game — had referred him to the Old Pro. What Paul received was nothing he had hoped for but everything he had needed: the Ultimate Mulligan and the gift of a second chance in his own son's life.

Life is full of mulligans, thought Paul with a smile. *I used to detest the term, but now "mulligan" is one of the sweetest words in my vocabulary.*

That night he made a special entry in his journal.

•   •   •

You think I would have seen this coming and have been prepared for it, but the idea of the Old Pro dying never crossed my mind.

I feel numb.

I will miss him every day.

I just know I will see him sitting in a rocking chair on the porch of the Royal and Ancient when I get to heaven someday. I can't wait.

Something else happened today that caught me off guard. I think I became an Old Pro. This kid, Tim, wants to spend time with me. He thinks I know a lot about life and he wants to learn from me.

I feel like Jesus, my caddy, guided me to Tim. I actually feel like there is a chance I could impact his life, in some small way—the way Will Dunn impacted mine.

I was so amazed by the number of people the Old Pro knew and touched. People from every walk of life gathered to remember him. Maybe God could use me like this in the lives of others. Here is my prayer.

Jesus, you are my caddy. I am stepping onto a stretch of the course that is unfamiliar. I can't be an Old Pro unless you guide me and give me wisdom. Please help me as I walk with Tim. I am going to miss the Old Pro. Thank you for his life. Thanks for what he meant in my life and to so many others. I want you to know that I am available to help others learn about who you are and the mulligan you offer that can change their lives. Amen!

AFTERWORD

WHEN THE TWO OF US MET, we immediately became soul mates and friends because we had a couple of important things in common. First, we both love golf and have played and enjoyed the game ever since we could walk. We never met a golf game we didn't like. To us, the worst a golf game can be is fabulous. Second, we both love Jesus — not as someone trapped in a church, but as our friend and Savior who wants to walk with us both on and off the course.

The Mulligan brings these two loves together in a special way.

First of all, it is not something that you deserve or can earn. Someone else has to give it to you. You can't just take a shot over in golf because you want to. The people playing with you have to say, "Why don't you take a mulligan?"

Second, you have to be willing to receive it. Sometimes people's egos get in the way and they say, "Nah, forget it. I'll play it where it lies." Receiving a mulligan is not easy. And yet, if we're humble enough to accept it, we begin to realize our true potential.

We hope you have learned through this book that we have a friend in Jesus who is ready to forgive us with a mulligan and still loves us when we goof. The more we walk with him and let his love manifest in us, the fewer mulligans we will need and the more we will start to live better lives, just as Paul did, because we don't want to disappoint him or ourselves. We don't think Paul could have learned that on his own. He needed Willie Dunn.

Have you had any Old Pros in your life—wise mentors who have taken you under their wing? Norman Vincent Peale was that for Ken. When Norman was eighty-six years old, he and Ken began to work together on *The Power of Ethical Management* (William Morrow, 1988). Norman kept on nudging Ken toward a relationship with Jesus. He said, "Ken, the Lord has always had you on his team. You just haven't suited up yet." That became his rallying call for Ken to realize that God was waiting for him with the greatest mulligan of all time.

Wally had three Old Pros: Duke Dupree, a club champion from Indiana; Harvey Penick, legendary golf pro and author of *Harvey Penick's Little Red Book* (Simon & Schuster, 1992); and Davis Love Jr., a renowned golf instructor who was tragically killed in a plane crash. All three of these men guided Wally in the development of the characters and story line for this book.

If you would like to know more about how to begin this journey or pass *The Mulligan* on to others or join in fellowship with like-minded folks in your area, please contact us at www.wallyarmstrong.org. Wherever you are on your spiritual journey, you will find some thought-provoking words of wisdom from the Old Pro on our website, as well as information on how to get additional copies of the book and other Old Pro resources.

If you are interested in Ken's *Lead Like Jesus* ministry, go to www.LeadLikeJesus.com.

It was a joy for us to write *The Mulligan*. We hope the book not only improves your golf game but changes your life as well.

Ken Blanchard
Wally Armstrong

ACKNOWLEDGMENTS

THE WRITING OF A BOOK goes way beyond the thinking of the authors. Mentors like the Old Pro come into our lives all the time to help guide our journey. We've already mentioned Duke Dupree and Harvey Penick in the afterword as influential people in Wally's life. Davis Love Jr. had a significant, positive influence on both of us. We would be remiss not to acknowledge a few other people whose thinking, cheerful support, and encouragement helped bless *The Mulligan*.

WALLY ARMSTRONG
WANTS TO ACKNOWLEDGE:

Jim Hiskey and Doug Coe for keeping my focus constantly on the simplicity of the gospel — Jesus, Jesus, Jesus.

Owen Matthews, Jack Smith, Bill Stephens, and Ander Crenshaw for demonstrating to me throughout the years that life is truly all about relationships.

Steve Deihm and Dave Robie for their coaching and friendship and for freeing me up to write and teach.

Jack Keesling, Dr. Joe Miller, and coach Conrad Rehling for being Old Pros to me and significantly impacting my life as a young golfer.

Al McDonald for his mentorship and for sharing great insights of writing wisdom.

Joe Girzone, writer of the "Joshua" series of books, for his inspiration in using parables to creatively teach about the MASTER.

Tim Philpot for his deep, heartfelt love for God and for the original concept of a mulligan for golf and life.

Brent Sapp for his friendship and help in the development of the Old Pro's character.

Dr. David Cook for teaching me the mental truths of golf: "see it, feel it, trust it."

My mother, Lois, for her love and encouragement throughout the years.

KEN BLANCHARD
WANTS TO ACKNOWLEDGE:

Chuck Hogan and Lynn Marriott for what they taught me about the difference between playing "golf swing" and playing golf and about how important focus is in golf and in life.

Bill Hybels for teaching me how to create a personalized journal and helping me realize that I can't follow through or keep my commitment to God without help. I must accept and receive his grace by faith and not by my deeds.

Robert S. McGee in his book *The Search for Significance*, for teaching me that our self-worth is not a function of our performances and the opinions of others.

James Dodson in his book *Final Rounds*, for helping me realize the potential of NATO golf.

Norman Vincent Peale for what he taught me about the power of positive thinking in every part of our lives.

Jim Ballard for sharing the need for all of us to enter our day slowly.

Henry Blackaby for his insight into how God talks to us in a unique way.

Bob Buford for teaching me about the final exam and that Jesus makes up the difference between us and a hundred. What a wonderful way to teach about grace.

Bob Toski, my coauthor for the *Golf Digest* article "The One Minute Golfer," as well as **Tom Wischmeyer, John Darling, Dave Emerick**, and all the great teachers from the Golf University for all they taught me about the wonderful game of golf.

Keith Jackson, the great NFL tight end, for sharing with me that BIBLE can stand for Basic Instruction Before Leaving Earth.

Art Turock for teaching me the difference between interest and commitment.

Michael O'Connor for teaching me about how important it is for organizations to have rank-ordered values.

Tony Robbins for teaching me what the brain and the computer have in common.

John Ortberg for sharing with me how absurd the term "alarm clock" is.

WALLY AND KEN
WANT TO ACKNOWLEDGE:

Zondervan Team Members who worked on the book and the related curriculum products: **Dudley Delffs**, Senior Vice-President and Publisher for Trade Books; **John Raymond**, Vice-President and Publisher for the Church Engagement team; **Greg Clouse**, Senior Editor for curriculum products; **Verlyn D. Verbrugge**, Senior Editor at Large for Biblical and Theological Resources; **Rob Monacelli**, Creative Director for Ministry Resources and Church Engagement; **Ben Fetterley**, Interior Book Designer and Project Coordinator; **Mike Cook**, Marketing Director for Church Engagement team; **Tom Dean**, Senior Director for Marketing; and **TJ Rathbun**, Director for Audio and Visual Productions.

The late **Bob Jewell** for catching our vision for *The Mulligan* and being willing to organize and implement a strategy to make it happen through Old Pro Resources.

Phil Hodges for all his encouragement, feedback, and help throughout the writing of this book.

Phyllis Hendry and all the Lead Like Jesus staff for praying for us and cheering us on.

Kevin Small for his feedback on the book, work on the contract, and all his creative marketing thinking.

Richard Andrews for all his help on our contract and for making this book a reality.

Nancy Jordan for putting our ramblings down on paper in a loving, caring, and encouraging way.

Anna Espino, Dottie Hamilt, Martha Lawrence, and all the great people at the Ken Blanchard Companies who have been so patient and helpful to us throughout this project.

Debbie Armstrong and Margie Blanchard, our wives, for their love, patience, and inspiration to press on with *The Mulligan*.

And finally, last but not least, to **Jesus** for making it all possible. To You be all honor and glory. Amen.

About the Authors

Ken Blanchard, coauthor of *The One Minute Manager*®
and more than forty other management and leadership books, is universally characterized as one of the
most insightful, powerful, and compassionate people in
business today. He is known for his knack for making
the seemingly complex easy to understand. Ken is Chief
Spiritual Officer of The Ken Blanchard Companies™, a
global leader in workplace learning, employee productiv-
ity, leadership, and team effectiveness. He is a cofounder
of Lead Like Jesus, an organization to help all people
learn and model the leadership principles that Jesus lived.

Walter Armstrong has competed in more than three
hundred PGA Tour events worldwide, gaining a lifetime
membership to the PGA Tour. He now travels the world
speaking and conducting clinics for charities and corpo-
rations, as well as producing videos, clinics, and books
on golf technique. Armstrong has coauthored six books,
including *In His Grip*, *Playing the Game*, and *The Heart
of a Golfer*.

ADDITIONAL RESOURCES

BOOKS

Wally Armstrong. *In His Grip: Foundations for Life and Golf.* Woodstock, VT: Countryman Press, 1998.

Ken Blanchard. *It Takes Less Than One Minute to Suit Up for the Lord.* Mechanicsburg, PA: Executive Books, 2004.

Ken Blanchard and Phil Hodges. *Lead Like Jesus.* Nashville, TN: Nelson, 2005.

Ken Blanchard and Phil Hodges. *Lead Like Jesus: Leadership Development for Every Day of the Year.* Nashville, TN: Nelson, 2008.

Ken Blanchard and Phil Hodges. *The Most Loving Place in Town.* Nashville, TN: Nelson, 2008.

James Francis, with foreword by Ken Blanchard. *One Solitary Life.* Nashville, TN: Nelson, 2005.

Ken Jennings and John Stahl-Wert. *The Serving Leader.* San Francisco: Berrett-Koehler, 2004.

WEBSITES

Lead Like Jesus is a nonprofit ministry with a mission to inspire and equip people to Lead Like Jesus in order to restore joy in work and family. For more information on Lead Like Jesus and its products, services, and programs, please visit:

www.leadlikejesus.com

Wally Armstrong conducts exhibitions and clinics worldwide. His website showcases golf instructional products, information about golf schools, and a host of Mulligan-related offerings: *The Mulligan Study Guide* and *The Mulligan 6-DVD Study Guide*; special discounts on Mulligan tee gifts; information on Mulligan golf retreats and starting a Mulligan Golf Club in your area, and international travel opportunities. To schedule Wally at your next event or find out about sponsoring a Mulligan Open golf event, please visit:

www.wallyarmstrong.com

Related Products
The Mulligan Study Guide and *The Mulligan 6-DVD Study Guide*, available from Zondervan.

Share Your Thoughts

With the Author: Your comments will be forwarded to the author when you send them to *zauthor@zondervan.com*.

With Zondervan: Submit your review of this book by writing to *zreview@zondervan.com*.

Free Online Resources at
www.zondervan.com

Zondervan AuthorTracker: Be notified whenever your favorite authors publish new books, go on tour, or post an update about what's happening in their lives at www.zondervan.com/authortracker.

Daily Bible Verses and Devotions: Enrich your life with daily Bible verses or devotions that help you start every morning focused on God. Visit www.zondervan.com/newsletters.

Free Email Publications: Sign up for newsletters on Christian living, academic resources, church ministry, fiction, children's resources, and more. Visit www.zondervan.com/newsletters.

Zondervan Bible Search: Find and compare Bible passages in a variety of translations at www.zondervanbiblesearch.com.

Other Benefits: Register yourself to receive online benefits like coupons and special offers, or to participate in research.

ZONDERVAN®

ZONDERVAN.com/
AUTHORTRACKER
follow your favorite authors